THE ABCs of
CONTAINER SHIPMENT

(2nd Edition)

Photo by Ian Taylor on Unsplash

Rupnarayan Bose

The ABCs of container shipment

Cover design: Siddhartha Bose

SUBJECT INDEX

BOOKS BY THIS AUTHOR:

- *Letters of credit - Theory and Practice*,

- *Understanding Trade Finance through Q&A and case studies*

- *Beyond Trade Finance*

- *All about UCP 600 (Second Edition)*

- *Fundamentals of international banking*, Macmillan, 2007 (2nd Edition)

Non-fiction:

- *A postcard from East Africa*

THE ABCs of CONTAINER SHIPMENT

Author's Note

Confession, Acknowledgement and Disclaimer

As with any industry, the import and export trade has its own language and terminologies that are peculiar to itself. The industry uses words and phrases to describe processes or equipment that may make little sense to the layman or when applied out of context. Within this universe, transportation of cargo occupies a special place. It's a world by itself. Unless one is conversant with the jargons related to this industry, one may not understand what these terms and acronyms really mean. For the uninitiated, it could mean a big risk.

Like a few of my fellow bankers, I too have been completely ignorant as far as transportation and logistics in general, and container transportation in particular, were concerned. This was simply because there was no apparent motivation to dig deeper, to know more. My job did not demand it. No one made me aware of it. Ignorance was bliss. But there comes a time in every man's life when he reaches a crossroads. He has to choose – whether to continue to remain a frog-in-the-well, or tap the fountains of knowledge, seize the available opportunities to learn and to grow.

I finally decided to tackle the issues that I had carefully avoided all these years and to make some sense of them. This book represents that exercise, a compilation of the information that I wanted to assimilate, understand and absorb. It's a work-in-progress.

Some of the issues that I have attempted to address and find answers to (not always successfully, though) relate to the following:

♦ The functions of port, seaport, dry port, berth, quay, pier, jetty and a CFS;

♦ Understanding terms such as LCL, FCL, CFS, CY, FIOS, the liner terms and many more;

♦ The differences between container depot, container yard, container port and container terminal;

♦ How a container moves from the seller/exporter to the buyer/importer – the stages;

- ♦ 'Delivery' in the context of container shipment vis-à-vis the Incoterms 2020 rules.

Through a series of short questions at the end of this book, I have attempted to structure as a refresher the issues related to container shipment, hoping that these will help to cement the basics in the mind of the reader.

Let me admit that this is not an original piece of work. In the quest for knowledge, the information in this document was put together from several published sources, with a little bit of editing thrown in for better readability, logical flow and comprehension. I owe it to Hariesh Manaadiar for clarifying many of the basic concepts associated with container shipping. To all the original authors and owners (whether mentioned by name or not) of their respective work, my sincere appreciation and thanks. There was no intention to usurp their rights or their privileges. My sincere apologies if one feels that I have.

Moving on, here is what Bob Ronai, an acknowledged expert in trade finance and transportation, had to say:

> "Every BL covering container shipment, whether FCL or LCL, is in fact a multimodal BL because the carrier takes charge of the goods at a CY or CFS, and this argument is of course supported by Incoterms 2020. So why do banks continue to use the outmoded requirement for an "ocean" or "marine" BL? *Only because they are largely unaware of the actual logistics of international trade.*" (Emphasis added.)

A similar question could be asked about the banks' requirement in their documentary credits for "clean, on-board bill of lading" for a container shipment. Or about stipulations in the documentary credit about transhipment being allowed or not. Transhipment is practically unavoidable when goods are shipped in containers. Once again, is it lack of awareness alone?

Since transport documents are integral part of their lives, bankers should sit up and explore these issues in greater depth. So should the others involved in trade finance who are yet to understand "the actual logistics of international trade". Be aware of at least the basics.

This is my effort in trying to make sense of the jargons that populate the cargo transportation business, to understand the basics of container shipment, the terms specific to trade finance, transport documents and the Incoterms rules (including the meaning of 'delivery', especially in the context of container shipment.

This is a completely revised and expanded version of the first edition. Yet it scratches only the surface of the vast world of cargo shipment. If it motivates you to study the subject further, or proves helpful to better understand the subject, the purpose of this author in compiling this edition would have been served.

If any reader wishes to add to it or improve on it, he/she is most welcome to revert with suggestions. Corrections and feedback, too, are definitely welcome.

Stay healthy. Enjoy life.

Rupnarayan Bose
rnbose@gmail.com

27-March-2022
Revised: 21-July -2024
Updated: 25 April 2025

CHAPTER 1

INTRODUCTION TO
CONTAINER SHIPMENT

1.1   LINERS AND TRAMPS

Merchant marine[1], whether privately or publicly owned, are the commercial ships of a nation. The term merchant marine also denotes the personnel that operate such ships, as distinct from the personnel of naval vessels. Merchant ships are used to transport people, raw materials, and manufactured goods.

Merchant shipping includes cargo ships, passenger ships, and tankers. Merchant ships are classified by their operating methods. One of the two principal types of merchant ship is the ocean liner; the other is the tramp steamer.

---

[1] Source: https://www.britannica.com/topic/merchant-marine

A liner operates on a regular schedule of designated ports, carrying whatever cargo and passengers are available on the scheduled date of sailing. A vast fleet of liners, ranging from passenger-cruise vessels to refrigerated cargo ships, continue to cover the world.

The tramp steamer (or tramper), in contrast to the 'liner', operates without a fixed schedule, going wherever required to deliver its cargoes. The tramp is a descendant of the early merchant ships whose masters (who were also their owners) loaded them with cargo at home to sell abroad, and vice versa. Tramp vessels are sometimes available at short notice to load various cargoes from any port to any other port. This flexibility makes them ideal for transporting cargoes that do not adhere to regular shipping schedules. Tramps are used mainly for carrying bulk commodities or homogeneous cargoes in whole shiploads, with each voyage separately negotiated between the ship's owner and the shipper, usually through a broker[2].

Incidentally, the term "tramp" is not to be misunderstood in a derogatory sense. The term "tramp" is just an industry identifier because such ships do not have a fixed home (route/port), and is free to wander (sail) around the world in search of cargo fixtures or carrying cargo. Tramps are classed by reputable classification societies and may use an open registry or Flags of Convenience (FOC). Additionally, both types of vessels are covered by

---

[2] https://www.britannica.com/technology/tramp-steamer

reputable Protection & Indemnity (P&I) clubs and operated by crews with the necessary expertise to handle operations and voyages.

Cargo ships can be either liners, or tramps. Some of the newer types of cargo ships are bulk carriers, which transport ores or other dry cargoes in bulk; container ships, which handle standardized containers in a highly mechanized fashion; and roll-on, roll-off ships, which handle cargoes through their bow or stern ports. Passenger ships include ocean liners (which have now largely been supplanted by jet aircraft for transoceanic travel), cruise ships, and ferries. Tankers are used to transport crude oil, oil-based fuels, and natural gas.

In the third quarter of 2020, the economy best connected to the global liner shipping network, as measured by the LSCI (liner shipping connectivity index)[3], was China. Singapore, the Republic of Korea, the United States of America and Malaysia followed next in the rankings. Over the last ten years, the rank order among the most connected economies remained almost unchanged, with China far ahead of the others.

As of 05 January 2022 Mediterranean Shipping Company (MSC), a privately-owned organisation founded in 1970, had evolved from a one-vessel operation to become the world's largest container

---

[3] LSCI indicates a country's position within global liner shipping networks. It is calculated from the number of ship calls, their container carrying capacity, the number of services and companies, the size of the largest ship, and the number of other countries connected through direct liner shipping services.

shipping line. MSC owns, charters, and operates 4,284,728 TEUs and 645 ships calling at 500 ports on 230+ trade routes, carrying around 23 million TEUs annually using a modern fleet, equipped with the latest green technologies.

1.1.1 Conference liners

Association of fleet owners which has a definite route of sailing and definite days of touching a particular port, whether the vessel is fully loaded or not vessel will sail in pre-determined route and itinerary. Under this arrangement, two or more shipping lines come together to provide scheduled cargo and/or passenger service on a specific trade route under uniform rates and common terms.

1.1.2 Common carrier

In shipping, common carrier is described as one which offers carriage to the public generally without restriction. A common carrier generally cannot discriminate between shippers and must offer identical and identically situated cargo to be carried on the same terms.

1.2 CHARTER PARTY[4]

It's an agreement between a vessel owner and a charterer which provides for the terms under which the charterer may use or

---

[4] https://www.bbc-chartering.com/terms/glossary?q=liner+terms

employ the ship. Charterer is defined as the party who charters the vessel from the owner under the terms of the charter party.

The three most prevalent types of charter parties are:

(1) *Time charter* under which the charterer hires the vessel (including the crew) from the owners for a period and pays hire charges for the use of the ship. Time charter parties set out the terms and restrictions to the time charter, including cargo type and quantity, accessible ports etc. Responsibility for the technical operation and navigation of the ship stay with the master and owner. (See also Time Charter Party)

(2) *Voyage charter* under the owner agrees to carry the charterer's cargo from particular port(s) to other destination port(s). Voyage charter party is a contractual document for the carriage of goods by sea, outlining the terms between charterer and ship owner, for the use of the ship's cargo space. Under this type of charter, the ship owner or carrier is responsible for the operating costs of the ship.

(3) *Demise or bareboat charter* under which the charterer hires the vessel but provides the crew and vessel management.

1.3   HOW DO YOU MEASURE UP?

Reverting to ports, harbours and their performance, an UNCTAD (2020d) Review of Maritime Transport 2020[5] United Nations publication Sales no. E.20.II.D.31 offers some interesting insights

---

[5] https://unctad.org/webflyer/review-maritime-transport-2020

while analysing the "Time at port by market segment in the top 20 economies by port call, 2019." The review shows that the economy which recorded the most port calls of ships in 2019 was Norway. On average, cargo-carrying ships departed from Norwegian ports *within one half day after their arrival.* That's amazing in terms of turn-around time and performance.

Such high efficiency and the extremely low turn-around time indicate that the backward and forward integration at the ports, the infrastructure, the human capital etc. must be of very high order. Such performance underlines the fact that all segments of the supply chain move smoothly, in tandem, perfectly synchronised to achieve this, day in and day out.

It is for the other ports around the world to set this as their benchmark and work out how they can best improve their efficiency and move towards achieving, if not surpass, this level of performance.

You too may like to find out how the major ports of your country rank vis-à-vis the above. The information is important since the efficiency at the ports is a significant indicator and has a major impact on the economy of the country as a whole.

CHAPTER 2

HARBOUR, PORTS AND TERMINALS

2.1 INTRODUCTION

As we all know, every vocation, trade or profession has its own specialised practices and procedures peculiar to it. These peculiarities include terminologies that are characteristic of and specific to that particular trade or profession. It is necessary for us to understand the precise meaning or application of these terms if we are to properly comprehend the nuances of a particular trade.

This book is about transportation of cargo, with special focus on container shipment. The terms have been selected for inclusion in this book keeping this in view. The terms related to these areas are explained in the next few pages of this chapter[6].

When it comes to commercial operations, there may be a hierarchy to the terms that we use.

A general guideline is as follows:

- A coastal country (contrary to one that is landlocked) may have many harbours

- Each harbour may have several ports

- Each port may have multiple terminals (dedicated for specific purposes)

- Each terminal may have berths and/or quay which is where all the commercial actions take place.

A terminal is a part of a port, and refers to the specific part of a port dedicated to a certain type of activity, such as container terminals or bulks.

There is no hard and fast rule about how a place is described. In many instances in different countries, these different terms are used interchangeably. There are still more terms like wharf, dock etc. that are used to refer to a berth or harbour.

---

[6] Source: *Difference between harbour, port, terminal, berth, quay, pier, jetty*
by Hariesh Manaadiar, May 10, 2021.

2.2   HARBOUR

A harbour is an in-use location with good draft and tranquil sea with natural or man-made barriers like breakwaters towards main sea/ocean thus safeguarding the shore from extremes of high/low tidal activity and peak effects of storm. A harbour provides a ship with safe anchorage and allows the transfer of goods and/or passengers between the ship and the shore. A harbour needs to have the draft necessary for bigger ships to enter and exit, while also providing enough space for the ships to turn and pass each other.

Natural harbours are usually surrounded by land and this creates a protective bay making it a good anchorage point for ships. Apart from coastlines around the world, natural harbours may also be found along fjords, coves, lake sides, lagoons and estuaries. Many of these natural harbours have been improvised upon, to be able to handle commercial activities.

Since natural harbours were not always exactly at the location or of the type required, artificial harbours are developed for the purpose of trade and commerce. Some hallmarks of artificial harbours are breakwaters, concrete walls (sea walls) and other forms of barriers designed to protect the harbour from storms or reduce the tidal range.

2.3   PORT

Port comes from the Latin word portus, meaning "gateway", "haven" or "harbour." Ports are points of convergence between two geographical domains of freight and passenger circulation – the land and maritime domains. In other words, a port is a place where water and land meet. Therefore, there are trains and trucks that come into the port for the purpose of loading of cargo on to a ship or for its unloading from a ship.

It may be defined as a town by the sea or by a river that has a harbour, or the harbour itself. On a ship, the port side is the left side; starboard being the right-hand side of a ship.

When the harbours are used for the purpose of commerce and trade such as loading and unloading of cargo, passengers or anything that generates revenue, these harbours may be said to serve as a port.

Thus, a port is a place within the harbour where a ship can dock for a commercial purpose of either handling cargo or passengers or taking care of the ship's requirements. A harbour may have many ports owned by different business, government, cooperatives, and scientific bodies.

A port may have various terminals provided with customized facilities and design specific for handling various types of cargoes. These ports may be classified based on the cargo that they handle.

Airports are the counterpart of sea ports, meant for serving transportation of freight and passengers by air. Unlike a sea-port where the interface is between sea and land, the interface for airports is between land and air.

2.4   TERMINAL

You may have noticed that mostly passengers and freight cannot travel *individually*. They do so in batches or groups. To put it in another way, their transportation happens in batches – not as and when a person or a consignment arrives at a terminal. A single flight or train, or even a bus, carrying x number of passengers at one go. Terminals are central and intermediate locations in the mobility of passengers and freight where passengers and freight assemble or disperse, described as any location where freight and passengers either originate, terminate, or are handled in the transportation process – but invariably in groups or batches. One core attribute of transport terminals, therefore, is their convergence function. They are obligatory points of passage having capitalized on their geographical location which is generally intermediate to commercial flows.

Terminals could also be the points of interchange within the same modal system, or points of transfer between modes. While some of the ports may handle only specific cargoes, a vast majority of the ports around the world handle multiple cargoes within the same port – once again, to maximise opportunities. These demarcated areas handling different types of cargoes are known as "terminals". Terminals often require specific facilities and equipment to accommodate the traffic they handle.

A single port could, thus, have the following types of terminals:

- ◆ Container terminal (details coming up later)

- ◆ Bulk cargo terminal

- ◆ Oil & gas terminal

- ◆ Ro-Ro (Roll On-Roll Off) terminal (popularly also known as car terminal)

- ◆ Multipurpose terminal

Terminals may have one or any of these open yards, godowns (warehouses), cold storages, tanks, silos for storage of specific commodity, cargo. Loading and unloading, handling, storage, security, documentation and custom clearance are specialised key components of terminal services at a port. To help distant onshore clients / customers, port business entity or govt. may create one or many extended cargo storage, identification, handling, documentation, custom clearance services at clearly demarcated yards, godowns (warehouses) at inland locations near export/import centres, or in and around cities called inland terminals.

A terminal may have many berths either along the shore ground (like a wharf) or extended in sea called jetty berth. Jetty berth are connected to shore land through jetty approach. Jetty and jetty approach can be used as pier as a specific use case. Normally in each harbour, around which sea-fishing is common, one such pier jetty is common sight where small boats and trawlers are moored with the pillars of the jetty.

The term 'Terminal' is also extensively used to identify inland locations to where goods are transported from the port using rail and road modes, or from where cargo is transported outwards.[7]

Good example are Inland Container Depots (ICD) which are custom bonded depots/terminals also referred to as "Dry Ports" because some of them are still under control of the main port authority or ports and terminal operator.

Pix: Jetty

[Oil ships may not come to berths. They may moor near single or double point mooring buoy tied to sea bed by permanent catenary anchors a few kilometres from the sea shores. Moorings are connected with undersea pipeline to the shore. A ship connects with floating hoses to mooring to transfer oil to tanks in onshore

---

[7] More info available at: https://transportgeography.org/?page_id=104

terminal through mooring buoys and undersea pipeline. The operation is done through tug boats.]

2.5   FREIGHT TERMINAL

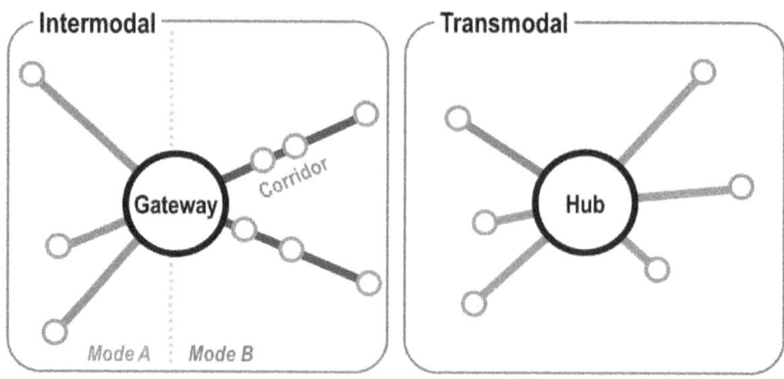

Freight handling requires specific loading and unloading equipment. In addition to the facilities required to accommodate ships, trucks, and trains (berths, loading bays, and freight yards respectively) a very wide range of handling gear and storage are required, which is determined by the types of cargo handled. Freight transport terminals have a set of characteristics linked with core (terminal operations) and ancillary (added value such as distribution) activities. The result is that terminals are differentiated functionally both by the mode involved and the commodities transferred. A basic distinction is that between bulk (liquid bulk and dry bulk), break-bulk[8], general cargo, and containers.

A feature of most freight activity is the need for storage. This produces the need for terminals to be equipped with specialized

---

[8] Refer to section 3.9.

infrastructure such as grain silos, storage tanks, refrigerated warehouses, or simply space to stockpile such as for containers or bulk commodities. In addition, a variety of transloading activities (defined at section 11.13 in this book) can take place in the vicinity of terminals, particularly if long-distance inland transportation is involved. Transloading, when suitable, helps to reduce transportation and inventory costs.

2.6   BERTH/QUAY

A berth is basically an area where the ship is moored onto the bollards and where the cargo is loaded or discharged on and off the ships. The land area surrounding the berth is also sometimes referred to as a quay depending on where you are from.

Each port or terminal provides for several berths/quay which usually has shore equipment for handling cargo, covered sheds, open cargo storage areas etc. where the cargo is discharged, loaded and may be stored if required. One container port can have several berths/quay where several ships can be handled at the same time.

2.7   PIER, JETTY

The word 'jetty' is derived from the Old French 'jetee' – a projecting part (synonyms: pier, dock, wharf, mole). In English it's something similar to jutting out. Jetty is a wide stone wall or wooden platform where boats stop to let people get on or off, or to load or unload goods. Pier and jetty are pretty similar in their purpose - which is usually to tie up small boats or yachts. Originally a pier or jetty meant a walkway extending into the sea/ocean where people could take a walk, do some fishing, eat at the restaurants etc. Usually no heavy commercial activities or cargo loading/unloading happened at a pier or jetty.

But this definition has changed. A jetty may also be a long projection into the sea to allow coal vessels, oil tankers etc. to load without needing a deep-water port adjacent to land. For example, a liquid cargo jetty is being built at JNPT, Mumbai, India to provide birthing space to ships carrying liquid cargo like POL, LPG, edible oil, molasses and chemicals. The terminal features two liquid cargo berths and a capacity of 4.50 MMTPA. When fully commissioned in 2025, it will be capable of handling all types of liquid cargoes. The terminal will be equipped with 19 pipelines of different sizes varying from 8" to 24" diameter connected from jetty to tank farms (see pix next):

Courtesy: https://www.jsw.in/infrastructure/jsw-jnpt-liquid-terminal-private-limited

Pix: Solid Products Jetty, Malaysia (https://www.aurecongroup.com/)

Oil jetty, Mauritius Port Authority (http://www.mauport.com/faq-page)

2.8   CARGO

This word originates from the Latin word *carricare* which means "to load on a cart, or wagon". Nowadays it's loaded on something much bigger. The word cargo or freight refer to goods or produce carried by a carrier (ship, road, rail, air) by water, air or land– generally for commercial gain. The term "cargo" now covers all types of freight, including that carried by rail, van, truck, or intermodal container transport.

A cargo ship or freighter is a merchant ship that carries cargo, goods, and materials from one port to another. Thousands of cargo carriers ply the world's seas and oceans each year, handling the bulk of international trade.

Cargo may also be transported by cargo plane, also known as a freighter. It is an aircraft specifically designed and optimised to transport goods and cargo rather than passengers.

Containerised cargo, general and break bulk cargo account for about 70.2% of global trade. Wet bulk such as tanker cargo (crude oil, petroleum products and gas) of about 29.8% accounts for the balance.

More about cargoes – including those about unitised cargo, wet bulk, break bulk and dry bulk cargo, liquid bulk cargo and out of gauge cargo (among others) – are coming up shortly.

2.9   FREIGHT FORWARDER, CLEARING AGENT[9]

2.9.1   Freight forwarder

A freight forwarder is a multi-function agent/operator who undertakes to handle the movement of goods from point to point on behalf of the cargo owner. The key function of a freight forwarder is to ensure that the cargo is picked up from the seller and delivered to the buyer, using the most suitable resources and routing possible at the required place, at the right price and in the same condition that it was picked up from its origin. A freight forwarder or a clearing agent saves the seller and the buyer the trouble of arranging documentation, negotiating freight contracts, monitoring the movement of the cargo, transportation, customs clearances, port inspections and all related activities.

While in many instances a freight forwarder and a clearing agent may be the same entity, they could be different entities too.

A well-established freight forwarder is expected to have the following capabilities (either owned or outsourced):

- experience in all modes of transportation – road, rail, air and sea

- able to provide cost-effective and efficient cargo shipping solutions based on the customer's requirement

---

[9]   https://www.shippingandfreightresource.com/freight-forwarder-and-clearing-agent/

- able to arrange storage, distribution or "forwarding" of the cargo as per the instructions of their client

- have the capability to negotiate freight rates with the shipping line

- able to book cargo with the shipping line as per the requirement of the client or under their own contract

- process all relevant shipping documents such as certificates of origin, customs and port documentation, bills of lading and associated shipping/negotiating documentation (Eur1, Certificate of Origin, etc.)

- issue their own approved house bill of lading (HBL) although they are not an NVOCC

- arrange transportation of the cargo between the customer's premises and the port

- have a thorough knowledge of cross-border cargo movement

- acts as a carrier in cases where they issue house bill of lading

These capabilities may be owned or outsourced. However, they

- may or may not also do customs clearance

- may or may not be accredited to customs, port etc. and cannot do customs clearance if not accredited.

2.9.2   Clearing agent

A clearing agent is essentially one who specifically takes care of the customs clearance aspect of the business for goods entering or leaving a country. Compared to a freight forwarder, a clearing agent is more specific to the country where they are based, ensuring compliance with import/export regulations, thus facilitating the smooth flow of cargo across international borders.

Every country has its own set of regulatory requirements relating to customs but one common requirement is that the clearing agent or customs broker (as they are referred to in a few countries) have to be accredited with the local customs authorities, border agencies, port and other authorities relevant to the shipment of goods. They should have a valid clearing licence at the time of clearing the goods on behalf of the customer.

CHAPTER 3

ABOUT MARINE CARGO

3.1   TYPES OF MARITIME CARGO[10]

Maritime cargo may be divided into two broad groups, for example:

a) General cargo (unitised cargo): Which includes (i) break-bulk, (ii) neo bulk, and (iii) containerised cargo;

b) Bulk cargo (loose cargo): (i) dry bulk, and (ii) liquid bulk.

The following paragraphs describe them in a little more detail.

The packaging used inside containers to transport in and out of containers either consists of pallets[11] (or skids), which are often

---

[10] https://transportgeography.org/?page_id=10258

[11] See section 3.4

wooden or plastic supports for the load, often shrink wrapped, slip sheets made of plastic, or crates.

3.2   GENERAL CARGO

General cargo refers to goods that are of many shapes, dimensions, and weights – such as machinery, processed materials, and parts. Because the goods are so uneven and irregular, handling is difficult to mechanize. General cargo is possible to being loaded on to general, non-specialized stowage areas or standard shipping containers e.g., boxes, barrels, bales, crates, packages, bundles, and pallets. In order to lift general cargo, it is often packaged on pallets, in crates or racks. General cargo handling is labour intensive.

3.3   UNITISED CARGO[12]

Manufactured products and perishable goods come in a variety of shapes and sizes, often with considerable storage constraints. These can be very diverse, covering forest products, metals and metal goods, machines, electronics, food chemicals, raw materials and consumer goods among others. Consequently, these cargoes need to be treated very differently compared to free-flowing dry bulk cargoes, like grain.

Imagine having to individually move the millions of computers and computer parts transported around the world every year. It would be a logistical nightmare. Instead, these 'units' are packaged

---

[12] https://www.maritimeinfo.org/en/Maritime-Directory/unitised-cargo

together as unitised cargo before transportation. While the terms unitised and containerised are often used interchangeably, strictly speaking 'unitised', as a cargo type, includes containers as well as a number of other modes of transportation, such as pallets, barges, closed wagons, goods trailers and trucks.

In shipping, unitization usually consists of grouping cargo together, such as onto a pallet, then wrapping and loading it into a larger container for shipping. The bigger units are created so that these can be handled more easily by a machine such as a forklift.

This terms, therefore, defines cargo secured to pallet or skids (see next), or when the individual component shipping packages are banded or otherwise securely held together to form a single unit that has been prepared by the shipper and which can be handled with mechanical forklift equipment as one unit.

3.4   PALLETS

A pallet[13] (also called a skid) is a flat transport structure, which supports goods in a stable fashion while being lifted by a forklift, a pallet jack, a front loader, a jacking device, or an erect crane. It is the structural foundation of a unit load, which allows handling and storage efficiencies. Pallets are generally made of wood, but can also be made of plastic, metal, paper, and recycled material.

---

[13] **More info at:** https://www.inboundlogistics.com/articles/types-of-pallets/

Although pallets come in all sizes and configurations, all pallets fall into two very broad categories: "stringer" and "block" pallets.

For shipment using containers, goods are often placed on a pallet secured with strapping, stretch wrap or shrink wrap and shipped. In addition, pallet collars can be used to support and protect items shipped and stored on pallets.

3.5　BULK CARGO

The term "bulk" relates to trades where the cargo is carried in loose form, (i.e. the cargo is not packed) and loaded directly into the holds of the ship. Bulk cargo is classified into two groups as follows:

- *Solid or dry bulk cargo*: These include a combination of small particles or dry cargo such as food, flour, bulk grains, coffee, agricultural products, stones, stone chips, materials etc. These types of bulk cargo are transported in large quantities on board a ship.

- *Liquid bulk cargo*: These include commodities such as petroleum, chemicals, water, crude oil, etc., which are transported by tankers, ships or trains.

The ships that carry these bulk cargoes are known as bulk carriers, ore carriers or bulkers and may be classified on the basis of their deadweight tonnage (DWT)[14].

Bulk goods may be delivered "free out", i.e. when the cargo is presented by the carrier at the arrival port for unloading while still in the cargo holds – the unloading being handled and paid for by the buyer. It may also be on 'free on board' terms – depending on what the seller and the buyer agree on. (See "liner terms", chapter 5.)

3.6 DRY BULK CARGO, SOLID BULK CARGO[15]

The nature of dry bulk cargo is opposite to that of liquid bulk. The range of solid bulk cargoes is considerable. These include major bulk commodities like iron ore, coal, grain, alumina, fertilisers, scrap, sugar, sulphur, cement etc. and minor bulks (forest products and the like). Ship types that are meant to transport the cargo may vary from dedicated bulk carriers to general cargo vessels and a large range of 'coasters'. Transportation from the port of destination to inland reception facilities is almost exclusively carried out by inland barges and coasters.

---

[14] Refer to section 6.12
[15] https://www.maritimeinfo.org/en/Maritime-Directory/dry-bulk-cargo

Coasters primarily operate in and around the coastline or within the exclusive domestic waters of a country. Coaster vessels navigate easily through shallow waters, sharp bends, and inland waterways. Their role is not merely restricted to ferrying goods across the nation. Coasters act as a part of the essential supply chain that supplies countries and allow trade to flourish.[16]

These products (dry bulk) have two features in common: (a) they are unpacked, and (b) are homogeneous. These two properties make it easier for dry bulk cargo to be dropped or poured into the hold of a bulk carrier. These are, therefore, loaded direct from the transport that brings the cargo to the port on to the carrying vessel using grabs, suction and conveyors or from silos and similar facilities at the wharf.

As the name suggests, dry bulk cargoes need to be kept dry. Any moisture that finds its way into the cargo could ruin the entire load, at considerable cost to the ship owner.

It may also be surprising to learn that many dry bulk cargoes are classified as 'Dangerous Goods' requiring special attention during loading, transportation and discharge since, (a) they could shift during shipment, causing ship instability, or (b) because of their inherent nature such as being explosive when mixed with water, or (c) being dangerous to the marine environment.

---

[16] For more on 'coasters' visit https://www.marineinsight.com/types-of-ships/what-are-coaster-vessels/.

3.7   LIQUID BULK CARGO

These free-flowing liquid cargoes, which include crude oil, liquefied natural gas (LNG), chemicals, gasoline, fruit juices and vegetable oils are not boxed, bagged or hand stowed. Instead, they are poured into and sucked out of large tank spaces, known as the holds, of a parcel tanker. Liquid bulk cargo is loaded on to, and off-loaded from, a cargo carrier using pumps and pipelines.

3.8   NEO BULK

This type of cargo has some characteristics of bulk and some characteristics of break bulk cargo, for example logs, automobiles and steel. It includes cargo where each pre-packaged unit is accountable such as lumber (bundles), paper (rolls), steel, and vehicles (numbers). The mode of loading and unloading is lift-on/lift-off or roll-on/roll-off. The movement of these vessels often are a little off the routes of major shipping lanes.

Each of these types move by specialized ocean vessels. Car or vehicle carriers are in no way similar to vessels carrying logs, and cannot be interchanged. Vehicle carriers are generally multi-racked, provided with ramps for vehicles to roll up to the ship or roll down to the berth and require less water depth as the density of the goods is less. In contrast, log carriers carry on their open holds and require greater draft as the goods are dense. The logs are difficult to handle at all points, i.e., at yard, berth and on board the ship, resulting in longer turn-around time (TRT) of ships.

These ships are smaller in size than the container vessels because of the difficulty in handling of goods.

Stacking of logs in yards is not only time consuming but also accident prone as these are heavy cargo, whereas parking of cars are much easier. However, these are not stacked, and hence require large acreages of land. Compared to bulk cargo it is usually worth more on a per-kilo basis and it often moves on specialized ocean vessels.

3.9   BREAK BULK CARGO

Break bulk is different from bulk shipping used for cargo such as petroleum products (wet bulk) or grain (dry bulk). The term 'break bulk' was derived from the process of breaking down large consignments into smaller pieces to make it easy in the past to load on board ships.

'Break bulk' includes bulk cargoes that are non-unitised, non-containerised cargo and general cargo (vehicles, steel etc.). The expression refers to goods and general cargo that cannot be fitted inside a standard dry container due to size, shape, or weight. This includes oversized, irregularly shaped, extremely heavy, or hazardous goods requiring special handling. Today, it refers to any oversized cargo that cannot be shipped in containers or cargo bins, and have to be transported in the vessel hold or on deck.

Examples of break bulk cargo include construction equipment, manufacturing materials, oversized vehicles, boats, cranes, turbine blades, ship propellers, generators, large engines, trains, locomotives, yachts, boats, aircraft fuselages, bridge parts, windmill blades, tower sections, silos, tanks, boilers etc.

Such large and heavy cargo is often used in big industrial projects. That's why break bulk shipping and other types of special cargo can also fall under project logistics.

Although it's an effective method of shipping oversized cargo, break bulk shipping is more time-intensive than container shipping because each piece must be loaded and unloaded individually, hence is more costly. But, for many shippers, simply getting these large items from point A to point B via such a service, without dismantling the machinery (no deconstruction and re-construction), is a big plus.

The ships that carry these break bulk cargo are known as break-bulk, multi-purpose or general cargo vessels. These come in a variety of sizes and types such as single decker, tween decker, box holds. Cargo can be loaded under deck, on deck or between decks (tween deck) which some of the ships have. Such ships are typically "geared"[17] but may also be gearless.

In a break bulk or multi-purpose vessel, the cargo may belong to various customers. No dedicated berth or terminal is required.

---

[17] A "Geared" carrier is equipped for loading and offloading cargo at a port. It is not dependent on land based equipment. A "Gearless" carrier needs assistance from equipment installed at port.

3.10   OUT OF GAUGE (OOG) CARGO

Out of Gauge (OOG) or 'oversized' cargo (also referred to as AILs – abnormally shaped indivisible loads), describes any cargo that exceeds the dimensions of a shipping container by length, width, height or all of the foregoing. It defines any cargo that is extremely large or has unwieldy booms and protrusions that cannot be loaded into six-sided shipping containers simply for being too large or odd shaped. The term is a very loose classification of all cargo with dimensions beyond the maximum 40HC container dimensions. Instead, this type of cargo may be safely transported on a platform, flat rack, open-sided or in an open top container.

Some examples are very large automobiles such as luxury coaches, automobile trailers, aircraft parts, parts of wind turbines, construction machinery, abnormally large parts of machinery used in electricity generation, etc.

CHAPTER 4

CARGO CARRIERS

4.1   CARGO CARRIER VESSELS

Some of the most commonly used cargo ships are defined not necessarily by their size but by the purpose they are meant to serve:[18] An introductory description of each is furnished next.

4.2   GENERAL CARGO CARRIER[19]

A general cargo ship is extremely adaptable and can be used to transport virtually every form of dry, non-bulk cargo, from railway lines to agricultural machinery.

A distinct feature of general cargo ships is that they normally have their own "gear", which means that these versatile ships can cater

---

[18]   https://www.freightratecentral.com/blog/types-of-ships-used-to-carry-cargo

[19] https://www.maritimeinfo.org/en/Maritime-Directory/general-cargo

to smaller ports and terminals that do not have shore side loading and unloading equipment. And while these ships are often employed with abnormal loads that other ships may not accommodate (see "break bulk" or OOG), in lean times general cargo ships can easily turn their hand to carrying containers, bulk or bagged cargo.

4.3   BULK CARRIER

Bulk carriers or bulk vessels carry bulk commodities, or loose cargo like grain, coal, iron core, etc. (see foregoing). They come in a variety of sizes to suit the amount of cargo freight needing shipment. The ships that carry these bulk cargoes are known also as bulk carriers, ore carriers or 'bulkers'.

Bulk carriers have several cargo holds but a single deck. Cargoes may be loaded and carried as a single parcel with cargo in all holds for one customer or multiple parcels with cargoes in different holds for different customers. In that sense, cargo holds serve a commercially useful purpose. Dry bulk carriers are designed specifically to carry dry cargoes such as grain, iron ore and coal, in bulk.

Since bulk cargoes are mostly homogeneous but not packed or crated, it may require the use of dedicated terminals for the loading and/or discharging of cargo.

Types of bulk carriers:

a.   *Geared*: the carrier has its own cargo handling equipment in the form of derricks, cranes or conveyor systems. This means these ships can call at any suitable berth at the port for cargo operations.

b. *Gearless*: the ship doesn't have its own cargo handling equipment. These vessels make use of specialist port equipment to blow, grab, pump or convey the cargo away from the ship and into customised storage buildings. This means these ships can only berth at a terminal which has the required cargo handling equipment.

4.4   CARGO HOLD

While containers may be carried on conventional break bulk ships, cargo holds are specially constructed for dedicated container ships to speed up loading and unloading, and to keep containers secure while at sea. The hatch openings extend to the entire breadth of the cargo holds, and are surrounded by a raised steel structure known as the hatch coaming. On top of the hatch coamings are the hatch covers. Today, some hatch covers are made of solid metal plates that are lifted on and off the ship by cranes or by articulated mechanisms that are opened and closed using powerful hydraulic rams.

Another key component of dedicated container-ship design are the cell guides. Cell guides are strong vertical structures constructed of metal installed into a ship's cargo holds. These structures guide containers into well-defined rows during the loading process and provide some support for containers against the ship's rolling at sea. So fundamental to container ship design are cell guides that organizations such as the United Nations

Conference on Trade and Development use their presence to distinguish dedicated container ships from general break bulk cargo ships.

4.5   BREAK BULK VESSELS

Break bulk cargo vessels are known as break-bulk, multi-purpose or general cargo vessels. Break bulk vessels carry different types of goods that need to be loaded individually, like bagged cargo (e.g. cement, sugar, and flour), palletized cargo (e.g. paint, chemicals), timber, etc. They come in a variety of sizes and types such as single decker, tween decker and box holds. Cargo can be loaded under deck, on deck or between decks (tween deck) which some of the ships have.

In a break bulk or multi-purpose vessel:

- ♦ cargoes may belong to various customers,

- ♦ no dedicated berth or terminal is required,

- ♦ can operate from any free berth.

4.6   CELLULAR VESSELS

Container vessels are the most common mode of transport for shipments in containers, with the most common container sizes being 20', 40', and 45' in length. These types of vessels come in various capacities, and can carry a number of different types of cargo. A cargo vessel specifically designed to efficiently store and transport of freight containers, featuring vertical cell guides for securing and stacking containers one on top of the other, is called a 'cellular ship'.

Before 1991 most container ships were constructed with hatch covers. Because of the longer loading and unloading times of these types of ships, the cellular type was invented. As loading and unloading occurs only vertically and the containers have standardized dimensions (TEU), large quantities of cargo can quickly be loaded using gantry cranes.[20]

Container vessels are discussed in greater detail in chapter 6 in this book.

4.7   RO-RO VESSELS

Roll-on/roll-off ships are cargo ships designed to carry wheeled cargo, such as cars, trucks, semi-trailer trucks, trailers, and railroad cars that are driven on and off the ship on their own wheels or using a platform vehicle, such as a self-propelled modular transporter. The vehicles in the ship are loaded and unloaded by means of built-in ramps. The ro-ro ship is different from Lo-Lo (lift on-lift off) ship that uses a crane to load the cargo. The vehicles in the ship are loaded and unloaded by means of built-in ramps.

Since cars and trucks can drive straight on to the ship at one port and then drive off at the other port within a few minutes of the ship docking, it saves a lot of time of the shipper. It can also integrate well with other transport development, such as containers. The

---

[20] Wikipedia

use of Customs-sealed units has enabled frontiers to be crossed with the minimum of delay. Therefore, it increases the speed and efficiency of the shipper. It has also become very popular with travellers and holiday makers.

Ro-Ro vessels carry any type of wheeled cargo, typically automobiles and heavy machinery. There are various types of ro-ro vessels, such as ferries, cruise ferries, cargo ships, and barges. The ro-ro vessels that are exclusively used for transporting cars and trucks across oceans are known as Pure Car Carriers (PCC) and Pure Truck & Car Carriers (PCTC) respectively. ROPAX is an acronym for roll on/roll off a passenger. It is a ro-ro vessel built for freight vehicle transport with passenger accommodation.

The accompanying picture shows the front of a cross-section of an auto carrying ship. It carries vehicles of different dimensions and hence the deck levels of which can be adjusted. These ships are also called roll on – roll off (Ro-Ro) vessels when the vehicles instead of being handled using equipment are driven off the vessel through ramps connecting to the berths.

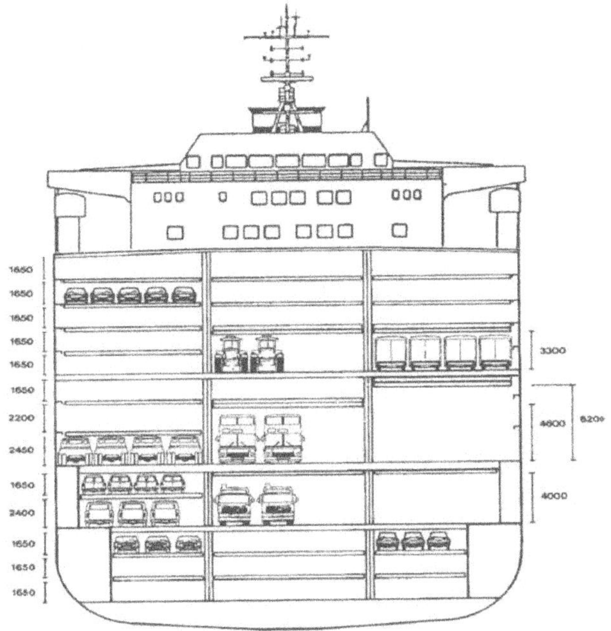

News flash

In January 2025 Chinese automotive company BYD Auto unveiled the BYD Shenzhen, the world's largest roll-on/roll-off (RoRo) vehicle carrier, capable of transporting up to 9,200 cars. The BYD Shenzhen measures 219 meters in length and 37.7 meters in width, with a draft of 9 meters. It boasts a maximum speed of 18.5 knots (approximately 34.3 km/h),[21]

---

[21] https://www.shippingandfreightresource.com/worlds-largest-ro-ro-ship-byd-shenzhen-ready-to-carry-your-vehicles/

4.8   SEA-FREIGHT LASH (LIGHTER ABOARD SHIP)

'Lighter Aboard Ship' (LASH) system refers to the practice of loading barges (lighters) aboard a bigger vessel for transport. It is a system of water transport. It was developed in response to a need to transport lighters – a type of (usually but not always) unpowered barge – between inland waterways separated by open seas.

Small ports sometimes can be inaccessible to container vessels, hence some of them carry on board their own barge (Lighter Aboard SHip). This is lowered outside such a port and the container lowered onto it for travel into that smaller port located up a river, inland. Some such inland ports have their own barges which go out to meet the container vessel off-shore. Lighters are typically towed or pushed around harbours, canals or rivers and cannot be relocated under their own power.

The barge itself is a boat with flat bottom developed for transporting goods through the rivers and canals that large vessels cannot go through. The typical size of a barge is measured at 195 by 35 feet and can load up to 1,500 tons of goods.

LASH vessels each carry about 70 LASH barges. The barges, all of a standard size with cargo capacity of 385 tons, are towed into ports and inland waterways to various shipping points where they are loaded with cargo and then returned to the ocean-going vessel. They are hoisted aboard by a special shipboard gantry-type crane and transported overseas where the process is reversed. LASH ships do not require special docks or terminals

4.9   MULTI-PURPOSE VESSELS

Multi-purpose vessels carry a combination of different types of cargo, and are very versatile – making them very popular vessels for cargo shipping. These are usually, but not necessarily, smaller ships with one or two box-shaped holds, reinforced tank top (15-20t/m^2) to allow heavy and project cargoes, often fitted with a removable tween deck. Multi-purpose vessels are built to transport various commodities: as general cargo in units, in bulk, or containerized including steel coils, timber and paper products, dangerous goods, etc.

4.10   REEFER VESSELS[22]

The term 'reefer' in shipping refers to refrigerated ships and refrigerated shipping containers that transport perishable commodities by sea. Reefer vessels carry goods that need to be frozen or temperature controlled. They commonly carry things like produce, meat, and fish. There are three different types of vessels used for the purpose of refrigerated shipping. These are as follows:

---

[22] More information on reefers available at
https://www.porttechnology.org/news/everything_you_need_to_know_a
bout_reefer_shipping/

- Ships that are used as multi-purpose vessels where the refrigerated part is below the areas reserved for passengers.

- Refrigerator ships that use the concept of refrigerated containers. Refrigerated containers are huge rectangular containers that are used solely for the purpose of cargo transportation.

- Ships that use specific ramps to load and haul the refrigerated cargo. These ships are the most common ones that are used in today's times.

4.11   TANKERS[23]

Carrying a wide range of cargoes – from gas and crude oil to alcohol and acids – the "tanker" family of ships include some of the world's largest mechanically propelled floating objects.

The Seawise Giant was a super-tanker that held the record for being the longest and heaviest ship ever built. It measured 1,504 feet in length and 225 feet in width, making it longer than the Empire State Building is tall. It had a deadweight tonnage of 564,763 tons, meaning it could carry more than 4 million barrels of crude oil. It was so large that it could not navigate the English Channel, the Suez Canal, or the Panama Canal.

It also had a huge turning circle of 1.86 miles, a draught of 25 meters and a stopping distance of 5.6 miles. The Seawise Giant

---

[23] https://www.maritimeinfo.org/en/Maritime-Directory/tankers

was not built for speed or manoeuvrability, but for sheer cargo capacity. The Seawise Giant's (renamed several times later on before being scrapped in December 2009) main purpose was to transport crude oil between the Middle East and the United States.[24]

Crude oil tankers, the largest of the group, carry oil from the oil producing countries, such as in the Middle East Gulf, to the refiners, such as North Europe.

Product tankers are the smaller sisters of the tanker family, carrying the oil that has been refined into oil products, such as gasoline or diesel. Other important members of the tanker family include chemical tankers, which are specially designed to carry corrosive acids and wines among other things, and gas carriers, moving methane and other gases in a liquefied or compressed state.

LNG carriers are specifically constructed in order to carry liquefied natural gases.

What makes the tanker fleet particularly special is its adaptability. Changing demands for its cargoes mean that there may be more business in one part of the world for one month, but that could switch dramatically the next month. Its responsive nature means

---

[24] Read the full story on it at
https://timesofindia.indiatimes.com/etimes/trending/this-is-what-happened-to-the-worlds-biggest-ship-ever-built/photostory/107731936.cms?picid=107731943

that ships can be switched between geographical areas to add or reduce capacity as the need arises.

4.12   TANKER SIZE[25]

Tankers come in seven general sizes:

- Approximately 20,000 - 30,000 DWT - Handysize

- Approximately 45,000 DWT - Handymax size

- Approximately 79,000 DWT - Panamax size

- Approximately 79,000 - 120,000 DWT - Aframax size

- Approximately 120,000 - 180,000 DWT - Suezmax size

- Approximately 200,000 - 300,000 DWT - VLCC (Very Large Crude Carrier) size

- Over 300,000 DWT - ULCC (Ultra Large Crude Carrier) size

The common rule is that the volume that can be carried in a tanker increases as a function of the cube of its length.

The Panamax size is the largest that can traverse the Panama Canal; the Aframax is the largest that can be handled by many ports and waterways; and the Suezmax size is the largest that can traverse the Suez Canal. The VLCC and ULCC "supertankers" are rarely, if ever, used for transporting any liquid other than crude oil.

---

[25] Source: Author Jayman0755; (https://www.funtrivia.com/trivia-quiz/World/Merchant-Shipping-210193.html)

Note that 60% of the world's oil is transported by ship, and over 99% of that arrives safely at its destination without causing significant environmental damage: most of the oil you see at the beach is an accumulation of fuel leaks from all types of vessels, not necessarily cargo leaks from tankers.

4.13   MARITIME NEWS

(A)

"China Delivers World's First Ultra-large Container Ship to CMA CGM", says a headline in MI News Network datelined April 16, 2025.[26] China State Shipbuilding Corporation Limited (CSSC) delivered a 24,000 TEU dual-fuel container ship, CMA CGM Seine, to the French shipping giant CMA CGM. The delivery took place in Shanghai. The CMA CGM Seine is the world's first ultra-large container vessel powered by both liquefied natural gas (LNG) and conventional fuel.

The ship is massive in size – 399 meters long and 61.3 meters wide, with a carrying capacity of 23,876 TEU containers, including space for 2,200 refrigerated containers. It can carry up to 220,000 tonnes of goods, and with an 18,600 cubic meter LNG fuel bunker, the ship is capable of sailing nearly 20,000 nautical miles without refuelling.

---

[26]   https://www.marineinsight.com/shipping-news/china-delivers-worlds-first-ultra-large-container-ship-to-cma-cgm/

(B)

Mediterranean Shipping Company (MSC), based in Switzerland, has reached a historic milestone by becoming the first container shipping company in the world to operate a fleet of 900 vessels. The company crossed the 900 mark with the delivery of MSC Germany, a modern LNG-powered container ship with a capacity of 16,000 TEU.

The new ship falls under the "maxi-neo-Panamax" category and is one of several similar ships joining the fleet in the coming months. This gives MSC a lead of nearly one million TEUs over its nearest competitor, Maersk. [27]

4.14 CRUDE OIL TANKERS, CRUDE CARRIERS

Crude oil tankers are designed to carry crude oil from oilfields to refineries around the world usually making the return journeys in ballast. The size of these ships increased steadily, peaking in the 1970s in order to bring economies of scale and the cost of oil transportation to the absolute minimum. The era of the supertanker, which commenced in the 1960s, quickly led to the construction of very large and ultra-large crude carriers (VLCCs and ULCCs), which are the biggest ships ever built.

As cargo-handling technology progressed, many tankers were generally fitted with steam coil heating in the cargo tanks to keep heavier grades of oil viscous and speed up the discharge of cargo.

---

[27] Source: https://www.marineinsight.com/shipping-news/msc-becomes-worlds-1st-shipping-company-to-operate-900-container-ships/)

They were also equipped with crude oil washing equipment for tank cleaning and inert gas systems to reduce the risks of fire and explosion.

4.15 SPECIALIST VESSELS[28]

Not all cargo can be as easily pigeon-holed and defined as containers, crude oil and dry bulk. Oversized, heavy or live cargo are transported from A to B. These specialist cargo have very different transportation requirements and the ships designed to transport more unusual loads fall into the broad specialist ship type. Known as Heavy Lift ships, these ships might be called on to transport products such as railway engines, giant container cranes for Ports and Terminals or wind turbines, as examples. These ships must be able to maintain stability while loading, moving and unloading these often extremely heavy cargoes. Some use ballast to counterbalance the weight, while others use hydraulic feet to clamp on to steady themselves on the quay.

Ships designed to carry livestock also need a specialist design to ensure that live sheep and cattle reach their country of destination in the best possible condition. Climate control, feed dispensers, watering equipment and equipment for the removal of manure needs to be considered and large quantities of bedding and food have to be carried.

Other specialised ships might include cement carriers, which carry no other type of cargo, and ice breakers, which keep the sea-lanes

---

[28] Source: https://www.maritimeinfo.org/en/Maritime-Directory/specialist

open throughout winter, providing safe passage for ships through ice.

4.16   AIR FREIGHT[29]

Air freight is often used for high value/low volume shipments. The traditional method of air dispatch is to deliver a consignment covered by an individual air waybill to an air carrier (either direct or through a freight forwarder). In the case of large loads, it is possible to charter a full aircraft or arrange for what is called a split-charter if the load will not fill the aircraft to full capacity.

Advantages of air freight

Faster delivery: Airports worldwide can be reached in 1 or 2 days or in a few hours by airfreight, thus reducing the risks of theft, pilferage or damage to the goods. Geographical reasons, time sensitiveness or perishable goods often rely on airfreight.

Better security: Airfreight has a tighter control over its cargo, thus it has better security that reduces the cargo exposure to theft, pilferage and damage.

Less packaging: Airfreight requires less packaging because of faster delivery and better security. Less packaging may mean saving freight, packaging and labour costs.

Lower insurance: Airfreight is faster and has better security than overland and ocean freight, thus the insurance premium rate generally is lower.

---

[29] UNDP Practice Series, Shipping and Incoterms, November 2008

CHAPTER 5

LINER TERMS

5.1   INTRODUCTION

'Liner Terms' is a bit confusing in that an individual term may be interpreted in a variety of ways at different parts of the world or by different ship owners/agents. You might call it the shipping companies' version of the "ICC Incoterms rules", designed to reflect their general conditions of sale (who pays for what?). However "liner terms" is not a standard term recognized by the ICC and it does not have any specific meaning or application in the context of Incoterms 2020.

Unlike the Incoterms rules, the liner terms are not standardised. Hence, what is meant by, say, 'storage' in the US may be interpreted differently in Singapore or the UK. Consequently, whenever one comes across a liner term, it is better to get a clear understanding of what the term precisely means before signing on the dotted line.

Another question is whether the usual "liner terms" and those applied specifically in charter-parties mean exactly the same thing, to be interpreted in the same fashion.

The 'Liner Terms' are from the perspective of the shipping line (i.e., *not* interpreted from the customer's point of view). That's why these are called 'liner terms'. These terms define services that are included and those that are not included in the amount charged as freight. It is worthwhile to remember, and as explained in chapter 1, any mention of 'line' or 'liner' refers to a regular, scheduled route for cargo transport between specific ports.

To understand the freight rate proposed by a shipping company, it is important to concentrate on the liner terms (more often, the two terms used in conjunction) between departure and arrival stations. Several combinations are possible. It is advisable to clearly define the extent of responsibility when quoting or accepting a quote on this basis. The acronym 'THC' represents terminal handling charges. A few of the more common liner terms are explained hereunder (the list is not exhaustive):

By the way, an important point to remember is that 'free' does not mean that it is "free" for the customer/shipper. Rather it is the opposite. *Free actually means 'not included' (in freight).* To put it in another way, whenever an item is 'free xx', the cost of that 'xx' operation is actually *excluded from the freight.* Someone other than the carrier is responsible for it and is required to foot the bill for that operation. Keeping this point at the back of our mind, let us examine the implication of a few of the more common liner terms. We begin with the stand alone terms before examining them when in combination.

5.1.1   Free In:

The freight rate covers the service offered by the company only after the container is aboard ship, stowed and lashed at the port of departure, but *excludes* the cost of loading goods onto a vessel (THCL). It means that the shipper is responsible for paying for the loading and for securing the cargo on board. The carrier is only responsible to bear the cost of the voyage.

5.1.2   Free Out:

Similar to Free In, Free Out indicates that the price of transport covers the merchandise only so long as it is aboard ship at the agreed port of destination. The merchandise is stowed but not unloaded from the ship. The consignee is responsible for the cost of unloading the cargo from the vessel at the destination. The term Free Out naturally excludes THCD, which is therefore not included in the freight rate proposed by the shipping company.

5.1.3   FIO, FI/FO (Free In and Out/Free In and Free Out):

Thinking coolly, it is easy to derive the meaning of these terms. The terms mean that the shipper is responsible for loading the cargo onto the vessel, and the consignee for the unloading process. Freight includes only the transport, but not the loading and stowing at the loading port, nor does it include unloading at the port of destination. Occasionally the shipper may also take the responsibility for unloading the cargo (but do check out the contract.)

5.1.4   FI/LO (Free In/Liner Out):

It is a shipping term for break bulk cargo, whereby the shipper is responsible for the loading of bulk cargo on to the vessel. The ship-owner (the line) is responsible for the transportation and unloading of cargo at the port of discharge. It is a logistics term that includes the freight rate of cargo and the cost of offloading as per the custom of the port, but as explained the loading of the cargo on board the ship is not included in the freight rate.

LIFO (Liner In/Free Out) is FILO in reverse.

5.1.5   FIOS (Free In, Out and Stowed):

It is a shipping term for break bulk cargo. This liner term stipulates that the cargo owner is responsible for the loading and stowing of the cargo, and the consignee is responsible for the unloading. The ship-owner (carrier) is responsible only for the transportation of the cargo.

Freight rates quoted on a FIOS basis specifically exclude all aspects relating to cargo handling operations. The ship is only responsible for expenses arising as a result of the ship calling into the port, i.e. tugs, pilots and light dues etc. Costs towards the loading, unloading or stowing of the goods on-board the ship are not included in the freight rate. These costs are payable separately by the shipper or the recipient as agreed between them.

Another important consideration when booking cargo on FIOS terms is that the ship does not bear any responsibility for the speed of loading or discharging. But these have a bearing on the overall operation.

5.1.6   FIOT (Free In/Out and Trimmed):

Generally used for break bulk shipment, this shipping term indicates that the shipper is responsible for the loading, and trimming of the cargo. (Trimming refers to the process of levelling and stabilizing cargo within a ship's hold to ensure safe and balanced transit.) In his turn, the consignee is responsible for the unloading. The vessel owner is responsible only for the transportation of the cargo.

5.1.7   FLT (Full Liner Terms):

The ship-owner is responsible for the loading, stowage, trimming, transportation and unloading of the bulk cargo. The cost of loading the vessel at the port, the stowage, and the trimming costs are included. The shipper is only responsible for delivering the cargo to the dock for loading. The cost of unloading the vessel at the port of destination is also included (in the freight rate quoted).

5.1.8   LIFO (Liner In/Free Out):

It is FILO in reverse. In the event of LIFO, loading the goods into the ship is included in the freight rate, whereas unloading is not. In this instance, the recipient of the goods at the place of destination must pay for unloading from the ship separately.

5.1.9   LILO (Liner In/Liner Out):

As the term implies, both loading and unloading of the cargo in and from the ship is the responsibility of the line and is included in the freight rate.

5.1.10   Gate In/Gate Out:

Freight and the usual surcharges are included in the rate, as are terminal handling charges at the port of departure and the port of arrival. It is a rate which is common for goods leaving Europe for the United States. It is widely and frequently used and requested by the major multinational groups which have close bilateral links with the major shipping companies.

5.1.11   Gate In/Free Out:

The freight and usual surcharges are included in the proposed rate, as is cargo-handling prior to departure (THCL – terminal handling changes loading). On the other hand, the cargo-handling at the port of arrival (THCD - Terminal Handling Charge Discharge) is not included in the freight quoted/charged. This combination is commonly used for goods leaving Europe for Asia.

5.1.12   Free In/Gate Out:

"Free In/Gate Out" (FIGO) in shipping terms means the freight rate *excludes* (meaning 'Free In') the cost of loading cargo onto the vessel, but *includes* the cost of cargo handling at the port of destination (Gate Out). The usual freight and surcharges are included in the shipping company's proposed price, as is cargo-handling at the port of arrival (THCL).

By way of a quick reminder let us reiterate that, in liner terms, when something is "free" it is for the shipper to pay or bear the cost for the same. The item marked as *"free"* is *excluded* from the freight rate quoted/charged. Caveat emptor.

5.2   WHO PAYS FOR WHAT?

Let us take CIF Incoterms 2020 to illustrate a specific point. The Incoterms 2020 rule A9(b) states:

> "(the seller must pay) the freight and all other costs resulting from A4, including the costs of loading the goods on board and transport-related security costs;"

Rule A9(c) of the Incoterms rules states:

> "(the seller must pay) any charges for unloading at the agreed port of discharge that were for the seller's account under the contract of carriage;"

The focus, therefore, is on the contract of carriage (including the liner terms?).

Rule B9(c) states,

> "(the buyer must pay) unloading costs including lighterage and wharfage charges, unless such costs and charges were for the seller's account under the contract of carriage;"

The above rule puts the issue squarely on the contract of carriage, it becoming a document of prime importance. It is now for the seller and the buyer to ensure that the liner terms (if used) in the contract of carriage and the Incoterms rules applied are in synch, pointing to precisely the same allocation of costs between them.

Where a transaction involves transport of cargo by sea under CFR or CIF Incoterms 2020 rules, and the seller opts for charter party contract (instead of using "Liner Terms" or similar non-standard term), both parties are advised to clarify loading and discharging costs together with other Terminal Handling Charges at the port of departure and destination in their contract of sales as clearly as possible.

CHAPTER 6

INTRODUCING CONTAINERS

6.1   INTRODUCTION

In 1956, Malcolm McLean created ripples in the cargo shipping industry by introducing the idea of container ships for the first time. The idea was the joint venture of McLean along with engineer and inventor Keith Walton Tantlinger. Tantlinger played a key role in the process of container standardisation, working extensively alongside the American Standards Association (ASA) and the International Organisation for Standardisation (ISO).[30]

Before the advent of containerization, break bulk items were loaded, lashed, unlashed and unloaded from a carrying vessel one piece at a time. It can be easily understood that by grouping cargo into containers, 1000 to 3000 cubic feet (28 to 85 m^3) of

---

[30] Source: https://www.seaspace-int.com/fun-facts-about-shipping-containers/

cargo, or up to about 64,000 pounds (29,000 kg) could be moved at a time. Containerization increased the efficiency of moving traditional break bulk cargoes significantly, reducing shipping time by 84% and costs by 35%. In 2001, more than 90% of world trade in non-bulk goods was transported in ISO containers.

A standard container is a metallic box (steel or aluminium) with a double door at one end and in which general cargo can be safely loaded and transported. Standardised containers have transformed the shipping and transport industry, allowing the transportation of goods by rail, road and ship with convenience, as the containers can fit onto different forms of transport with ease.

Containers allowed manufacturers to load goods at their factories and ship directly to stores and warehouses anywhere in the world without having to unload or reload while in transit, or to transfer their cargo along the way. This meant that manufacturing processes could be located far away from customers but still provide customers with an unimaginable variety of low-cost goods from across the globe, coupled with safety and security.

The standardisation of containers has helped increase efficiency and economies of scale. One is likely to come across a whole range of terms, acronyms and definitions on logistics – especially with regard to the movement of containers. This section makes an attempt to explain some of the commonly occurring terms in relation to container traffic.

But first, a few words about the global standards by which the containers are measured.

6.2   TEU

It is a standard of measurement of container size. It stands for Twenty-foot Equivalent Unit (TEU) – a universal standard used to measure a container and a ship's cargo carrying capacity therefrom. The internal dimensions of such containers measure about 20 feet long, 8 feet wide, and 8.5 feet tall. It can hold between 9 and 11 pallets, depending on whether they are standard pallets or EUR-pallets. Two TEUs (2TEU) have the capacity of a single FEU (Forty-foot Equivalent Unit).

The most common container lengths used currently are 20' (20-foot) and 40' (40-foot). Since 20' containers are the lowest common denominator and easier to calculate in relation to capacities and volume, the term TEU (which stands for Twenty-foot Equivalent Unit) has become an industry standard of reference. The container ships that carry these containers are designed and calibrated in terms of TEUs and the carrying capacity of a container ship is also defined in terms of TEUs. Since TEU refers to a 20', naturally a 40' container is considered as 2 TEUs because a 40' is twice the length of a 20'. The carrying capacity of container vessels are expressed accordingly.

6.3   FEU

Another standard of measurement of containers is where the container is slightly more than twice as long. Measuring 40-foot

(12.19 m), the unit of measurement is a Forty-foot Equivalent Unit (FEU). The 40-foot containers have found wider acceptance, as they can be pulled by semi-trailer trucks. The length of such a combination is within the limits of national road regulations in many countries, requiring no special permission.

6.4   CONTAINER TYPES

A container is one that can contain or hold. The shape, size or the volume of a container depends on the material it is intended to hold. The vast majority of containers are standardised steel boxes designed to hold any kind of cargo. These are mostly steel-framed and weather-proof boxes meant for the loading and transporting goods through various modes (land, sea, air and rail).

This is known as 'inter-modal shipping', because the cargo is almost always moved by more than one mode of transportation[31]. The very essence and role of shipping by container is to make freight transport easier, as well as to protect the cargo from the elements. With refrigerated containers (called reefers), they also ensure optimum conditions to keep the goods from degrading.

For shipment of cargo there exist about twelve different ocean shipping container types. In addition to the standard dry cargo container shipping containers are available in a variety of types – often referred to as "special" equipment. These special containers include open end, open side, open top, half-height, flat rack, refrigerated (known as "reefer"), liquid bulk (tank), and modular – all built to same exterior lengths and widths as the standard dry cargo containers.

Every container has its own unique unit number often called a box number, that can be used by ship captains, crews, coastguards, dock supervisors, customs officers and warehouse managers to identify who owns the container, who is using the container to ship goods and even track the container's whereabouts anywhere in the world.

---

[31] For this reason, all bills of lading (BL) issued to cover container transportation are actually multi-modal transport documents.

6.5   STANDARD SHIPPING CONTAINERS

The 20 feet and the 40 feet standard shipping containers are two
of the most widely used containers in the world to transport ocean
freight goods. The standard sizes of cargo containers (standard
lengths of 20 feet and 40 feet), also known as ISO containers,
allow them to be moved easily from truck to rail or ship. The dry
containers have small ventilator panels in the side panels and air
can enter/escape through gaps and holes in the floor panels as
well as through the door gaskets. These containers are not
equipped with cooling nor ventilation systems like the refrigerated
and ventilated containers. The 20 ft. standard shipping container
can hold up to 10 standard[32] pallets or 11 Euro pallets across its
floor base.

The standard shipping containers are also known as *dry shipping
containers or dry vans*. Standardisation of the containers has
helped in simultaneous standardisation of the supply chain and
increase in efficiency of transportation.

---

[32] It is important to note that no universally accepted standards for pallet
dimensions exist. Companies and organizations utilize hundreds of
different pallet sizes around the globe. While no single dimensional
standard governs pallet production, some sizes are so widely used they
become "standard", like the GMA (Grocery Manufacturers Association,
USA) pallet. The International Organization for Standardization (ISO) has
approved six pallet dimension which are now widely used as standard
pallet size around the globe.

6.6   OTHER TYPES OF CONTAINERS

Included among these are:

i.   Dry high cube (HC/HQ) shipping container,

ii.   Flat rack containers (Fixed End, Collapsible/Platform, Super-Rack),

iii.   Tank container

iv.   Bulktainer

v.   Side door container

vi.   Half-height containers

vii.   Open top shipping container,

viii.   Ventilated shipping container, and

ix.   Refrigerated shipping containers (also known as reefer containers).

Open tops fall within the category of standard containers, despite not having a roof. Unlike the flat rack, which also has no roof, open top containers have walls to protect the goods. These are used for easy loading of cargo such as logs, machinery and odd sized goods. The type of goods typically transported in open top containers is essentially the same as those being transported in flat rack containers, but with more irregular heights.

Flat racks*: Mainly used for cargo that exceeds the width (referred to as over-width) or height (over-high). If the cargo is just over-width or over-height, fixed-end flat racks can be used where the ends of the container are fixed and cannot be folded. Flat racks can be used for boats, vehicles, machinery or industrial equipment. Open sides may be used for vegetables such as onions and potatoes.

Collapsible flat racks or platform containers are those where the ends of the container can be collapsed to form a platform, and cargo is loaded on top of it.

Super-Rack containers are similar in use as a Flat Rack container but with a BIG difference. The difference is that in a Super Rack container, the corner posts can be extended upwards to increase the height. This is most useful when you have over-high cargo.

Tank containers transport many types of liquids such as chemicals, wine and vegetable oil.

Bulktainer: Normally has loading hatches on the top which enables bulk cargo to be poured into the container. These also have "gates" at the bottom of the container which enables the cargo to be offloaded by tipping the container rack.

Half-height containers: Half-height containers are shipping containers designed with a reduced height, roughly half that of a standard container, making them ideal for transporting heavy, dense cargo or in situations with height restrictions. These are well-suited for transporting items like pipes, tools, chains, anchors, hooks, and bulk materials such as coal, sand, and gravel. Some users feel that it is better in several respects to hire a 20-foot standard container and half-fill it rather than go for a half-height container. Loading, container handling, stacking etc. are among the reasons cited.

As the saying goes, look before you leap.

6.7   REEFER CONTAINERS

The term "reefer" was discussed in the context of reefer vessels under section 4.9. Here we specifically take up reefer *containers* for discussion.

These refrigerated containers do not *regulate* temperatures, they can only maintain them. In order to work, these must be connected at all times to an external power source such as the vessel's generator or the port's power supply. When booking a reefer container, it is important to make sure that necessary equipment is available throughout the entire international transport chain (from pick up to drop off) to help power the container and maintain its internal temperature. Reefers are often used to transport general cargo on the return leg as NORs (non-operating reefer).

6.8   CONTAINER DIMENSIONS

Apart from the OOG containers, most international container traffic – as already explained – is carried in either 20 foot or 40 foot containers. For the convenience of all parties concerned, the container dimensions are standardized. The maximum load is described in the following table.

Sea Freight Containers		
	20 foot container	**40 foot container**
Capacity (m³)	30	60
Internal dimensions LxWxH (meters)	5.89 x 2.32 x 2.23	12 x 2.32 x 2.43
Door W x H (meters)	2.30 x 2.14	2.30 x 2.23
Maximum load (tonnes)	18	30

Sea freight capacity, dimensions and load

In the last 65 years the ubiquitous shipping container has evolved from being just a dumb box to being a smart container capable of being tracked anywhere in the world, in some cases even to the bottom of the ocean.

Strangely, no one knows for sure how many shipping containers are there – grouped either under *total* number of containers, or under total number in *active duty* – in the world today. A general estimate is that around 65 million shipping containers are *in use* worldwide, served by a fleet of around 5,600 container ships. Over 17 million shipping containers are said to be in active circulation globally. In total, they make around 200 million trips a year. It is difficult to put a finger on the exact number since apart from international trade, containers are also used for storage, construction, and other purposes.

In 2019, 811 million TEUs of containers were handled in ports worldwide. The same year, ports in developing economies in Asia and Oceania handled 504 million TEUs of containers, accounting for 62 per cent of world port container traffic.[33]

Roughly 97% of the new shipping containers are said to be manufactured in China.

As per Alphaliner[34] (stats as on 22 Sep 2021):

a. 6,274 active ships were plying, of which 5,480 were fully cellular

b. Containers: 25,056,224 TEU of which 24,687,282 TEU were fully cellular.

Of these 24.44 million+ TEUs, 11.39 million+ TEUs are owned by shipping lines like Maersk (17.1%), MSC (16.6%), CMA-CGM (12.2%). Of these container shipping lines, Maersk owns the most amount of TEUs standing at 4.25 million+ TEUs.

6.9   CONTAINER IDENTIFICATION SYSTEM

Every container has its own unique unit number often called a box number, that can be used by ship captains, crews, coastguards, dock supervisors, customs officers and warehouse managers to identify who owns the container, who is using the container to ship

---

[33] UNCTAD Handbook of Statistics 2020 - Maritime transport

[34] https://alphaliner.axsmarine.com/PublicTop100/

goods and even track the container's whereabouts anywhere in the world.

The layout of the information on the body of a container is as shown in the picture below.

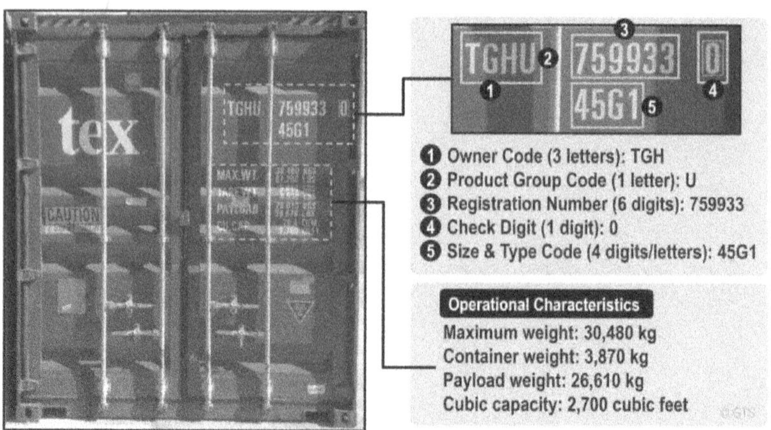

(Courtesy: The Geography of Transport Systems)[35]

6.10   SIZE MATTERS, BUT…

Container ships are cargo ships that carry the load in large-sized intermodal containers. They are classified into various categories based on their carrying capacity. Presently, there are seven major types of container ships in service. In ascending order, they are Small Feeder, Feeder, Feedermax, Panamax, Post Panamax, New Panamax (or Neo Panamax) and Ultra Large Container Vessel (ULCV). The record for the largest container ship, as of January 2024, is held by MSC's Irina-class, boasting a capacity of

---

[35]   https://transportgeography.org/contents/chapter5/intermodal-transportation-containerization/container-identification-system/

24,346 TEUs. One need to keep an eye on this, since the situation is very fluid. Newer and bigger ships are always in the pipeline.

Growth in the sizes of container vessels have a ripple effect – not always welcomed. The additional haul of TEUs may sound great but the problem lies elsewhere, possibly somewhere along the supply chain. To begin with, the ports lack the capacity to efficiently move the trade off the vessel to process it into warehouses and onto rails and roads. It's not always easy to do so.

Adding capacity on already congested trade lanes does little to solve the fundamental problems. The limiting factor is not the capacity on board the ships, but rather how many containers the ports and hinterland connections can manage, as well as the storage space in temporary container yards and at the final destinations[36]. A single bottleneck at any point along the supply chain has a ripple effect, thus choking the entire delivery process.

Another problem with these huge ships is the dramatic high rate of containers falling off large vessels. Because of the insatiable demand, large vessels are piled sky high at near-capacity in an effort to "speed up" delivery.

Mis-declaration of the weight of containers (refer to VGM next) is another issue. The dangers also range from stevedores incorrectly locking boxes on top of one another, to captains not

---

[36] https://www.freightwaves.com/news/evergreen-ever-ace-worlds-largest-container-ship-trade-solutions-viewpoint-lori-ann-larocco

deviating from a storm to save on fuel and time as they face pressure from charterers (the party who hires the vessel from its owner). If that pressure wasn't enough, add the effect of unpredictable weather and the causes become clearer.

Certain sea routes are also reputed for their extreme danger. The Drake Passage, for example, is the body of water between South America's Cape Horn, Chile, Argentina, and the South Shetland Islands of Antarctica – considered as one of the most treacherous voyages for ships to make.

The WSC Containers Lost at Sea Report (2023 Update)[37] reports that in 2022, 661 containers were lost at sea. This represents less than one thousandth of 1% (0.00048%) of the 250 million containers currently shipped each year, with cargo transported valued at more than $7 trillion. Reviewing the results of the total fifteen-year period surveyed (2008-2022), on an average 1,566 containers were lost at sea each year.

6.11   ABOUT VGM

The verified gross mass (VGM) is the combined weight of the *container* tare weight[38] and the weight of all cargo, including packaging and dunnage[39].

---

[37] https://www.worldshipping.org/news/world-shipping-council-releases-containers-lost-at-sea-report-2023-update
[38] Tare weight is explained in the next section.

[39] Explained at section 10.15.

VGM applies only to container shipment. Those who adopt the VGM requirement will not allow to load a packed container onto their vessels, unless a VGM has been provided by the shipper (who is named as such in the ocean bill of lading). If the VGM is not provided in due time, the container cannot be loaded.

The shipper is solely responsible for providing the VGM data. The shipping line and freight forwarder are not responsible for verifying if the shipper is supplying the right weight.

VGM is not applicable to break bulk shipment. Break bulk is exempt from the VGM requirement, *unless it is transported in a container*.

The VGM is declared separately from the gross cargo weight entered in the BL, and will not show on the BL.

From 01 July 2016, the VGM requirement was adopted by the International Maritime Organisation to increase maritime safety and reduce risks facing cargo, containers and all those involved in container transport throughout the supply chain.

The revised regulation was sought to be enforced globally, but countries may issue their own guidelines based on the SOLAS[40] requirement. (The SOLAS declaration[41] sets out minimum safety

---

[40] International Convention for the Safety of Life at Sea (SOLAS), 1974. For more information refer to
https://www.imo.org/en/About/Conventions/Pages/International-Convention-for-the-Safety-of-Life-at-Sea-(SOLAS),-1974.aspx

[41]   https://www.imo.org/en/OurWork/Safety/Pages/Verification-of-the-gross-mass.aspx

standards in the construction, equipment and operation of merchant ships. This may affect cut-off times, VGM tolerance allowance etc., which might differ from country to country.)

6.12   DWT

Dead Weight Tonnage (DWT) – a critical point of reference and a commonly used acronym – refers to the weight that a ship can safely carry. DWT includes the weight of the cargo on board the ship, the crew, stores, fuel, water, ballast etc.

6.13   TARE WEIGHT

In section 6.11 we briefly referred to container's 'tare weight'. It is the weight of a container when it is totally empty.

While many of us understand the common terms related to weight, let us be clear about the basic concept. Take, for example, oil packed in plastic drums made ready for sale. In this instance, the weight of the oil itself will be defined as the cargo *net* weight (of the goods being sold). When the oil is poured in a plastic drum and sealed, the weight of the oil plus the plastic drum together would be termed as the *gross* weight of the cargo. If these plastic drums are further packed in cartons, then the weight of the cargo (oil) plus the weight of the drum plus the weight of the carton containing the drums would give us the final *'cargo gross weight'*.

If the oil (in drums) packed into cartons are placed on pallets, then all these weights (including that of the pallets) put together will give us the revised 'cargo gross weight'.

A container is what is termed as a Cargo Transport Unit (CTU) used for the transportation of the cargo. It *facilitates* the movement of cargo. It does not form part of the cargo itself for sale, and definitely not included in arriving at the 'cargo gross weight'.

In the bill of lading, it is this 'cargo gross weight' that should be shown as the declared weight of the particular shipment.

CHAPTER 7

CONTAINER DEPOTS AND TERMINALS

7.1   CONTAINER TERMINAL

Every single shipment of cargo travels from point A to point B using several modes of transport – by rail, road, sea or by air. Containers are the only transport system that are used by all three modes of carriage (and relatively less by air). Shipment over sea is carried out on the container ships; similarly, rail and road transport of the containers is done by trains and trucks. Containers are transferred through container ports, terminals and depots.

The accompanying diagram (next page) beautifully illustrates the inter-relationship and inter-connectivity among the various players in this domain. The diagram explains how the containers move from the shipper to the buyer, using different modes of transportation.

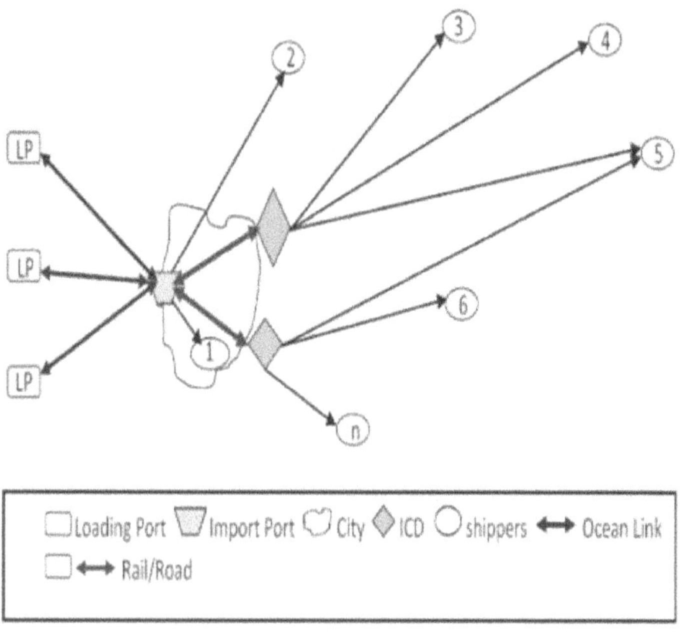

ICD connection to port and shippers/importers

Whenever a container is changed from one method of transport to another, it is referred to as 'changing the mode'. A container terminal is any location where this change takes place. For instance, a container that is being hauled on the roads by a truck may later be placed on to a train and travel by rail. If a shipment requires multiple mode changes on its journey, it will interact with multiple container terminals.

The container terminals around the world are classified with respect to their ownerships into five categories:

1. Public terminals,

2. Carrier-leased terminals,

3. Joint venture of the carriers and terminal operators,

4. Terminals that are operator-built and operated, and finally

5. Those which are built and operated by the carrier.

7.2 MARITIME CONTAINER TERMINAL[42]

Generally, a terminal is a facility where cargo containers are transhipped between different transport vehicles for onward transportation. The transhipment may be between ships and land vehicles, for example trains or trucks, in which case the terminal is described as a maritime terminal. Alternatively the transhipment may be between land vehicles, typically between train and truck, in which case the terminal is described as an inland terminal.

A maritime container terminal is a place where containers arriving by ocean vessels are transferred to inland carriers such as trucks, trains, or canal barges, and vice versa.

Maritime container terminals tend to be part of a larger port, and the biggest terminals of this type can be found situated around major harbours. Inland terminals serving containers tend to be

---

[42] https://www.container-transportation.com/container-terminal.html

located in or near major cities or industrial areas, with good rail connections to maritime container terminals.

7.3   MARITIME TERMINAL – STRUCTURE

In general logistics terms, container terminals can be described as open systems of material flow with two external interfaces. These interfaces are (a) the quayside for the loading of and the unloading from the ships, and (b) the land side, where containers are loaded and unloaded on/off trucks and trains. Containers are stored in stacks to facilitate the decoupling of quayside and land-side operation.

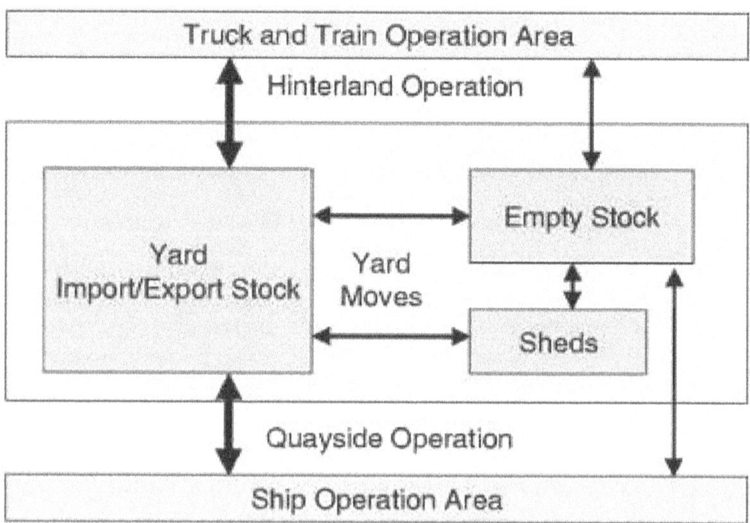

Fig: Operation areas of a container terminal and flow of transports

(Courtesy Larry, author, Viet Nam)

7.4   FUNCTIONS OF MARITIME TERMINALS

Every maritime terminal performs four basic functions. These are:

i.   *Receiving*:

   Receiving involves container arrival at the terminal, either as an import or export, recording its arrival, retrieving relevant logistics data and adding it to the current inventory.

ii.   *Storage*:

   Storage is the function of placing the container in a known and recorded location so it may be retrieved when needed.

iii.   *Staging:*

   Staging is the function of preparing a container to leave the terminal. The containers that are to be exported are identified and organized so as to optimize the loading process. Import containers follow similar processes, although staging is not always performed. An exception is a group of containers leaving the terminal via rail.

iv.   *Loading* – for both import (entering the terminal by sea and usually leaving by land modes) and export (usually entering the terminal by land and leaving by sea modes) containers.

   The *loading* function involves placing the correct container on the ship, truck, or other mode of transportation. In this work the emphasis is on internal logistics chain of container terminal (i.e. vessel-truck-yard and opposite direction respectively).

7.5   CONTAINER YARD (CY)[43]

Let us begin this section with a disclaimer, and remove a very important but a common misconception:

A container yard (CY) is NOT the place meant for the loading of cargo on to, or unloading of cargo from, a container. (If that be so, then where is it done? This question will be answered soon enough.)

Since a CY is *not* the place to handle the cargo inside a container, it has to be taken to a CFS (see sec.7.12). Alternately, the consignee – after completion of import formalities and payment of duties – perforce may take delivery of the whole container and take it away elsewhere (e.g. consignee's warehouse) for de-stuffing or de-consolidation. A small point to add is that after unloading of cargo, the container should be cleaned and returned within the permitted detention period to a mutually agreed place, else detention charges will be incurred.

It is very important to understand the precise functions of a container yard (CY). This understanding becomes particularly relevant when "delivery" under ICC Incoterms 2020 is discussed.

---

[43] https://www.navigatorlogistics.com/2018/01/11/the-difference-between-container-yards-terminals-depots/

Container yard (CY) means the enclosed area *within the confines of the terminal* used specifically for storage of container and chassis prior to vessel's loading or subsequent to vessel's discharge. Container Yard (CY) is a strictly regulated physical facility where,

(a)   containers are parked before loading on to the outbound vessel, or

(b)   after unloading from the vessel/ship on arrival at a port, for onward journey or immediate delivery to the consignees.

It is primarily a *transit station*, a facility where cargo containers are transhipped between different transport vehicles or modes, for onward transportation. The transhipment may be between container ships and land vehicles – for example trains or trucks – in which case the terminal is described as *a maritime container port*. Maritime container ports tend to be part of a larger port.

Alternatively, the transhipment may be between land vehicles, say between train and truck, in which case the terminal is described as an *inland container port*. Both maritime and inland container ports usually provide storage facilities for both loaded and empty containers.

Its main function being that of a transit station, a container yard (CY) is primarily used for FCL (full container load) shipment, not *LCL shipment.* (The goods cannot be loaded or unloaded individually here.)

Container yards, quite simply, are also areas of storage for empty containers. After a container has been deconsolidated at a depot (or unloaded directly by the importer), they are relocated to a yard where they are stored until their next assignment.

Container yards are also known as terminals and in limited occasions they may be placed outside of the port of loading or port of discharge.

7.6   ON DOCK CY[44]

The term 'On Dock CY' refers to a container yard that is situated *within the port area*. Containers are off-loaded from the ship and moved to the "On Dock CY" using straddle carriers or trucks and stored there till the receiver takes delivery of the cargo. Owing to the geographical location, storage costs are generally high (if not exorbitant) at an "On Dock CY", for which reason in some ports the full and empty containers are not allowed to be stored at an On Dock CY.

To avoid such high costs the shipping line moves the containers (on receiver's account and risk for full containers) to a nominated 'Off Dock CY' (ODCY) – described next – from where the receiver may take delivery.

---

[44]   https://www.shippingandfreightresource.com/difference-between-icd-on-dock-cy-and-off-dock-cy/

7.7   OFF DOCK CY

This term refers to a CY that is situated outside of the port premises but not necessarily inland. An Off Dock CY may be considered as an extension of the port subject to customs supervision and control, and to be treated like a container terminal inside the port in all aspects and subject to whatever additional requirements, rules and conditions which may be imposed by the Customs authorities of the country.

An ICD (inland container depot) may be termed as an Off Dock CY, but not all Off Dock CYs are ICDs. By definition, an Off Dock CY is *closer to the port* than an ICD. Thus, an Off Dock CY and/or ICD are different from an On Dock CY mainly in terms of the geographical location, size of operation and type of handling equipment used, but all may be functionally similar.

Traditionally, an Off Dock CY handles only Full Container Load (FCL) shipment. A similar facility handling "Less than Container Load (LCL)" shipment is termed as Container Freight Station (CFS). Coming up shortly – more on these terminologies.

7.8   CONTAINER DEPOT[45]

A container depot is an area where shipping containers are stored for transhipment. It serves as a holding facility for shipping containers, a transit point where containers are stored or held in transit once they are unloaded from the carrying vessel until it is

---

[45] Source: https://www.marineinsight.com/know-more/what-is-container-depot-purpose-and-design/

time for reloading for its onward journey. These container depots and yards are secure facilities that provide basic essential services for the container shipping companies. The depot is generally located inside a port or terminal or in the surrounding area. This enables for a quick and immediate transfer of containers between different locations.

A container depot can act as an extended part of the port like a satellite terminal and as a buffer for the terminals by storing empty containers. It is also a more affordable place to store containers than at the terminals at the port.

Container depots serve multiple uses and ensure a smooth flow of commerce between various countries and ports. One of the major issues that they solve is the holding of empty containers after unloading at the receiving party's warehouse. Another essential function of container depots and yards are the auxiliary services that they provide. These are in the form of cleaning, repair, maintenance, protection, fumigation, transportation etc.

Since containers are often kept at the depots for protracted periods of time entailing maintenance and frequent checks, the yard/depot provides a single place from where these services can be carried out. It is also an exchange market for importers and exporters to sell or buy container assets.

Storage facility for fully-loaded containers is not a container depot, but are merely holding facilities or terminals, and are temporary in nature since shipping companies aim at transferring the goods to the receiving party or to the care of the port at the earliest.

An important function of a container depot is the handling of LCL (by definition: Less than a Container Load) cargo. For an outbound journey, the cargo is delivered to a central facility, called a depot. Here, the freight is carefully packed and consolidated into a container (LCL cargo).

Likewise, when the shipment reaches its destination, it must pass through a depot, where the container is de-consolidated or de-stuffed back into individual packages, ready for pickup by the concerned consignee(s) after the payment of charges.

Besides container depots, there are also container ports and terminals. Container ports are those ports that primarily deal with the shipping of containers through carriers.

7.8.1 CONTAINER DEPOT SERVICES

a. Consolidation and deconsolidation of cargo;

b. Reefer storage facility;

c. Assist cargo owners with customs clearance, administrative and documentation procedures;

d. Provide temporary storage facilities for empty containers including reefers;

e. Arrange haulage cleaning, fumigation, maintenance and repair services;

7.9 OWNERSHIP OF CONTAINER DEPOTS

Container depots may be owned by the state, private or private-public. In Europe and North America, different parties take up ownership viz., port operators, rail companies, shipping companies. In Asia (India and China) these are mostly state-owned. The container depots in India are managed by the Container Corporation of India (CONCOR). ICDs in East Africa mostly fall under the private sector even though private-public partnerships are encouraged.

| Container depot | Container terminal | Container yard |

7.10 OWNERSHIP OF CONTAINERS

Whether owned or leased, collectively the containers owned and leased by *shipping lines* are called "carrier owned container (COC in short)" or line owned container. A VOCC (Vessel Operating Common Carrier – also known as Shipping Line) or an NVOCC (Non-Vessel Operating Common Carrier) is also classified as carrier who also owns/leases containers.

When a container is owned by the shipper, it is termed as a Shipper Owned Container (SOC in short). An NVOCC may also own and operate their own containers. Because they trade in many areas, it may be worthwhile for them to own their own containers. However, as far as the main carrier is concerned, for them a container owned by an NVOCC is still a "shipper owned container", because for a carrier, any container that does not form part of their owned, operated or leased fleet is considered to be a shipper owned container.

7.11   WHY WOULD A SHIPPER OWN A CONTAINER?

If it appears cheaper to hire a container, why should a shipper buy one? There are several reasons for that. At the same time, it is also important to consider who the shipper is. For a carrier, a BCO (Beneficial Cargo Owner – in other words a direct exporter), a Freight Forwarder or an NVOCC may be a shipper.

If the shipper uses a carrier owned container, the 'line' will need to charge the receiver *demurrage* and/or *detention* for keeping the container more than the allowed free time. Where the shipper/receiver knows that the cargo may need to be stored for a longer period, they may find it cheaper to buy a container, pack it and ship their cargo in it rather than use the carrier's own container and pay for demurrage and/or detention.

At remote projects, the receiver may not have the space or facilities to store the cargo and may use the container as a storage location. Additionally, in several projects, after unpacking, a container is transformed into a site office or living quarters for some of the on-site staff.

7.12   CONTAINER FREIGHT STATION (CFS)

Reference to CFS will come up very frequently as would that of CY. Therefore, it is very important for us to understand what exactly defines a CFS, and its characteristics and functions.

CFS refers to a warehouse where outbound cargo belonging to various exporters is 'consolidated' before being exported, or inbound cargo is 'deconsolidated' (unloaded from a container) before being allowed into the country of import.

Container Freight Stations are commonly found close to harbours, within terminals, close to massive warehouses or near major railway hubs. Container freight station (CFS) is mostly, but not necessarily, used for LCL (less than a full container load) shipments. The CFS is usually owned by a shipping line or a terminal and is responsible for customs examination and clearance procedures. Typical services include moving containers from a container yard, 'drayage'[46] of loaded containers, issuing shipping orders, stuffing, sealing and marking of containers as well as storage, sorting, stacking and preparing the containers internal load plan.[47]

---

[46] This, and several other terms that will keep popping up every so often, are explained later in this book.

[47] For more information refer to https://allcargologistics.com/container-freight-

Outbound cargo: A CFS is a warehouse where goods that belong to several consignors wishing to ship items get grouped together by a groupage operator (see sections 8.4 and 8.5 in this book). This is necessitated where the consignment by an individual shipper is not sufficient to fully load a container (FCL), or maximise the use of a container's capacity. Since it is not cost-effective to hire a complete container for a much less than a container load, the outbound goods are brought in by the individual shippers to a CFS to be weighed, custom-checked and consolidated (meaning assembled, stored or packed inside a container) before the containers are loaded on to the outgoing vessel/ship.

Inbound cargo: The inbound cargo (packed inside a container) after arrival at the port are taken to the CFS for custom clearance and 'de-consolidation' (the term means offloading and segregation) prior to delivery to the respective consignees. After payment of all THCs the goods are picked up by the designated consignee(s) and transported away using their own means of transport. ("Delivery" – as envisaged by the Incoterms rules – is thus possible at a CFS, not at a CY.)

A CFS is primarily a customs clearance centre. It takes the load off the ports. The CFS is operated for the receipt, forwarding, and assembling or disassembling of cargo. The CFS service may be necessary under any of the following circumstances:

---

station#:~:text=A%20CFS%20is%20an%20area,container%20load%20(
LCL)%20cargo.

- The kind of cargo and quantity of order does not warrant the use of the whole container. It is economical, therefore, not to hire an entire container only to fill and transport a much smaller load.

- The shipper's or the consignee's premises are inaccessible by container due to poor road conditions (e.g., narrow road, mud road, roads unable to bear a container load) or location (e.g., remote area not served by container).

- The overall load of vehicle exceeds the legal limits.

- The shipper or the consignee lacks the necessary container loading or unloading equipment. In other words, a CFS may be used by consignors where they do not have adequate arrangements at their own place for stuffing a container.

7.13   DRY PORT

Also called an inland port or intermodal hub, a dry port is very similar to a seaport but is located away from the sea port. It is an inland terminal connected to a seaport by rail or road. Dry port is a yard where containers; conventional bulk cargo and break bulk cargo are intermittently stored for consolidation, deconsolidation and customs appraisal, pending their export or import clearance, and is connected to a seaport by rail or road. Key features of an inland port are the transfer of containers between different modes of transportation (intermodal transfer) and the processing of international trade.

Dry ports are specialized facilities that are designed to process standardized shipping containers used in international transport. It consists of facilities like container yards, warehouses, railway sidings, cargo handling equipment, and administrative services for export import clearances. These inland ports often include storage facilities for a massive quantity of goods and are used for customs clearance of those goods. An inland port or dry port may also be linked to an airport or land border crossing rather than a seaport.

Dry ports act as a cost-effective distribution channel between seaports and high-capacity rail. One of the benefits of having dry ports is their ability to relieve the issues of storage and customs space that frequently plagues seaports. Another benefit is the ability of a dry port to speed up the movement of cargo between ships and inland transportation systems that distribute the goods.

Since the inland terminal is an extension of some port activities inland, the term "dry port" has gained acceptance and tends to be the most common term used. The term to define an inland terminal is subject to debate since many inland terminals are in fact 'wet' given their direct access to inland waterway systems. Moreover, the inland location can effectively be a port if a barge service is concerned, but fundamentally cannot be considered a port if it involves a rail terminal or more simply truck depots.

A similar issue applies to the inclusion of airport terminals, mainly their freight activities, as an element of an inland node. Thus, there seems to be no consensus on the terminology, resulting in a wide range of terms such as dry ports, inland terminals, inland ports, inland hubs, inland logistics centres, inland freight villages, etc.

Regardless of the terminology used, three fundamental characteristics are related to an inland node:

a.   An intermodal terminal, either rail or barge that has been built or expanded.

b.   A connection with a port terminal through rail, barge or truck services, often through a high capacity corridor.

c.   An array of logistical activities that support and organize the freight transited, often co-located with the intermodal terminal.

7.14   DRY PORT vs. CFS[48]

A Container Freight Station (CFS) situated away from sea where customs supervision is available is called a Dry Port. Exactly how far away from the sea is not defined. Dry Ports – sometimes also called an inland port or multimodal logistics centre – were created to reduce the congestion in seaports due to increased maritime transport of goods.

The exporter may complete customs formalities in CFS and ship the goods without having to transport the cargo to a sea port. Likewise, an importer may take delivery of cargo near his place

---

[48]   https://howtoexportimport.com/Any-difference-between-Dry-port-and-CFS--403.aspx

after completing procedures at a dry port. If the buyer insist for 'on board bill of lading' as a proof of export, the seller must wait for the shipment to reach the sea port and for the cargo to be loaded on the vessel, the on board bill of lading being issued thereafter by the shipping line. If the buyer needs only a proof of shipment, the exporter may obtain a 'Received for shipment Bill of Lading' from the carrier or its agent. Alternately, a seller may also receive a HBL from the groupage operator.

7.15   INLAND CONTAINER DEPOT (ICD)

Inland Container Depots, otherwise known as ICDs, are dry ports equipped to handle and temporarily stored containerized cargo as well as empties. An ICD is recognised by customs and port authorities as an extension of the sea port and customs officials are present in many ICDs. An ICD is, thus, "a common user facility with public authority status equipped with fixed installations and offering services for handling and temporary storage of import/export laden and empty containers carried under customs control and with Customs and other agencies competent to clear goods for home use, warehousing, temporary admissions, re-export, temporary storage for onward transit and outright export." (GoI)

ICDS helps hinterland customers to receive port services closer to their premises. Thus the customers get to process their shipments near their godowns (warehouses) and factories, away from the far-off ports. In doing so, ICDs help in de-stressing and decongesting the main ports where the storage spaces are usually limited.

Their primary purpose of ICDs is, therefore, to allow the benefits of containerization and customs formalities to be realized on the inland transport leg of international cargo movements. Containers are moved from the ship to the ICD and vice versa using rail and road networks.

7.16   FUNCTIONS OF ICD/CFS

a.   Receipt and dispatch/delivery of cargo.

b.   Stuffing and stripping of containers.

c.   Transit operations by rail/road to and from serving ports.

d.   Customs clearance.

e.   Consolidation and de-segregation of LCL cargo.

f.   Temporary storage of cargo and containers.

g.   Reworking of containers.

h.   Maintenance and repair of container units.

Import of goods through ICD: Customers who are based in the hinterland receive cargoes at ICDs just like the customers based in coastal areas receive cargoes at the seaport. Customers at ICDs undergo similar customs processes, inspections etc. like the coastal areas before receiving delivery of the container.

Export Goods through ICD: The exporters may take the goods to the ICD/CFS and file the Shipping Bill and other documents. The goods are examined by the Customs Officers, stuffed into the containers and the containers are sealed. The containers are then transported to the seaports (gateway ports) either by rail or road and loaded into the carrying vessels (ships).

7.17 DISTINCTION BETWEEN ICD & CFS

At both the places, the imported goods or export goods are ordinarily kept before clearance by the Customs. At both places, filing of Customs manifests, bills of entry, shipping bills and other declarations, assessment and all the activities related to clearance of goods for home consumption, warehousing, temporary admissions, re-export, temporary storage for onward transit and outright export, transhipment etc., take place. So what's the difference, if any?

The following[49] refers to the Government of India circular on the subject. (The set up with respect to other countries should be separately examined with respect to the country concerned.)

> Functionally there is no distinction between an ICD/CFS as both are transit facilities, which offer services for containerization of break bulk cargo and vice-versa. These could be served by rail and/or road transport. An ICD is generally located in the interiors (outside the port towns) of the country away from the servicing ports. CFS, on the other

---

[49] Source:
https://commerce.gov.in/writereaddata/UploadedFile/MOC_6364271962 99921726_Guidelines_setting_ICDs_CFSs_New.pdf

hand, is an off-dock facility located near the servicing ports which helps in decongesting the port by shifting cargo and Customs related activities outside the port area. CFSs are largely expected to deal with break bulk cargo originating/terminating in the immediate hinterland of a port, and may also deal with rail-borne traffic to and from inland locations.

Keeping in view the requirements of Customs Act, and the need to introduce clarity in nomenclature, all container terminal facilities in the hinterland may be designated as "ICDs".

The functional difference between an ICD and a CFS, as clarified in the Government of India notification[50], is as follows:

An ICD is a 'self-contained Customs station' like a port or air cargo unit where filing of Customs manifests, Bills of Entry, Shipping Bills and other declarations, assessment and all the activities related to clearance of goods for home use, warehousing, temporary admissions, re-export, temporary storage for onward transit and outright export, transhipment, etc., take place. (....).An ICD would have its own automated system ... with in-built capacity to enter examination reports and enable assessment of documents, processing of manifest, amendments, etc.

---

[50] Refer to GOI, Ministry of Finance, Central Board of Excise & Customs Circular No.18/2009-Cus. 8-6-2009.

A CFS is only a Customs area located in the jurisdiction of a Commissioner of Customs exercising control over a specified Customs port, airport, LCS/ICD. A CFS cannot have an independent existence and has to be linked to a Customs station within the jurisdiction of the Commissioner of Customs. It is an extension of a Customs station set up with the main objective of decongesting the ports. (Emphasis added) At a CFS only a part of the Customs processes, mainly the examination of goods, is normally carried out by Customs besides stuffing/de-stuffing of containers and aggregation/segregation of cargo. Thus, Custom's functions relating to processing of manifest, import/export declarations and assessment of Bill of Entry/Shipping Bill are performed in the Custom House/Custom Office that exercises jurisdiction over the parent port/airport/ICD/LCS to which the said CFS is attached. In the case of Customs Stations having facility of automated processing of documents, terminals are provided at such CFSs for recording the result of examination, etc. In some CFSs, extension Service Centres are available for filing documents, amendments etc. However, the assessment of the documents etc. is carried out centrally.

An ICD may also have a number of CFSs attached to it within the jurisdiction of the Commissioner of Customs just as in the case of a port and its CFSs (as on June 2009 there were 28 CFSs linked to Chennai port).

7.18   WAREHOUSE[51]

A warehouse is a commercial construction that is meant for storage of goods. Warehouses are used by manufacturer of goods, importers of commodities, wholesalers, people involved in transportation business, customs, etc. They are usually large plain buildings constructed in industrial areas of towns, cities and villages and have loading docks that are used for loading and unloading of goods from trucks. An open storage space, also termed as storage yards, generally store materials that can withstand the rigours of sun, rain and other weather conditions. Sometimes warehouses are so designed that they can load and unload goods directly from railways, airports or seaports.

Warehouses are usually equipped with cranes and forklifts for easy movement of goods that are generally placed on ISO standard pallets loaded into pallet racks. Warehouses that are equipped with large freezers for storage of food items that are perishable in nature are called 'Cold storages' or 'Cool warehouses'.

In India, warehouses are also referred to as 'godowns'.

---

[51]   https://www.mbaskool.com/business-concepts/operations-logistics-supply-chain-terms/15528-warehouse.html

CHAPTER 8

FCL, LCL AND RELATED TERMS

8.1   FCL AND LCL SHIPMENT

These two terms are commonly used in international logistics, regardless of the language. These are applied more to describe the shipper(s), the consignee(s) and their shipment, rather than the container's port of origin and termination. In both instances the intention is to despatch a full container load for cost effectiveness and in order to maximise the benefits. Then why two different terms for similar container loads? Read on.

8.2   FULL CONTAINER LOAD (FCL)

The expanded term for FCL is 'Full Container Load', yet it is a misconception that a container must actually be fully loaded for it to be called a FCL shipment. It need not necessarily be so. In reality, the term FCL (Full Container Load) is applied to a situation where the entire capacity of a single container is used up by a single customer for his cargo. It means that all the goods in that container are from a single shipper, is meant for a single consignee/notify party, and are covered by one B/L (bill of lading).

In shipping practice the term FCL, therefore, represents the fact that the whole container is booked by the shipper, the *single* consignor, or a forwarder on behalf of the consignee, exclusively for the transportation of the cargo of a single shipper. Even if the container is not completely full, the shipper would not be sharing the container space within with cargo booked by other shippers.

At the origin the FCL containers are usually packed by the seller at their premises. At destination these are unpacked at a place of the consignee's choice. An FCL may be packed by the shipper, or by a forwarder or another party contracted to do so. However, the shipper takes responsibility for the packing and is liable for the condition of the cargo packed in the FCL container. The costs are borne by that one party alone.

(Note: Which party does the packing has insurance implications. If any loss, damage or expense is attributed to bad stowage and if this stowage was performed by the seller, which will usually be the case with a FCL delivered to the carrier at the seller's premises, it may prove difficult for the assured to obtain any kind of indemnification. See Institute Cargo Clauses 'A', Clause 4.3 for more information.)

Advantages of FCL shipment:

(i)   It is a big help in door-to-door delivery;

(ii)   FCL shipping costs less than LCL shipment;

(iii)   FCL shipments offer a faster lead time/delivery because it need not stop at other ports for off-loading cargo.

(iv)   Once it is packed at the port of loading, it is not reworked anywhere and delivered 'as is' to the port of discharge. It may, however, be routed through a transhipment port in case there is no direct service from departure point to destination.

8.3   LESS THAN (A) CONTAINER LOAD (LCL)

The term LCL supposedly refers to any container shipment that constitutes less than a full container load (sometimes also referred to as loose container load, less than carload or loose carload – the word 'carload' referring to the rail car). But the term is misleading, and not exactly true. As with the term FCL, an LCL shipment may also carry a full container load. As with any FCL shipment, an LCL shipment too does not necessarily mean that the container must be 'full' – 100% or anywhere near its full capacity.

Instead, the term LCL is applied to a container that is loaded with goods from more than one shipper, each of whom has small consignments (less than a full container load, individually) to ship out. In order to make best use of the container space, and also to save on costs, it makes sense for the individual consignors/shippers to the same destination to share the same container capacity so as to *jointly* make up a full container load.

LCL transport is facilitated by a Non-Vessel Operating Common Carrier (NVOCC). NVOCCs reserve full containers from shipping companies based on traffic demand. They then proceed to offer space in the containers for small LCL shipments. The container space, as well as the container shipping costs, get shared with the other shippers. In that way, it makes economic sense.

It is important to note that the consolidation may be carried out by the shipping line themselves (which will issue their own B/L), or by a consolidator called a "groupage operator" (who will issue their HBLs to the respective consignors and later obtain a MBL – master bill of lading – from the shipping line towards its FCL shipment).

LCL (when consolidated by line): The shipping line collects these small parcels from various consignors/shippers and make up a Full Container Load. As the shippers are many, the shipping line would issue their individual bills of lading to the various shippers. These bills will be the direct line bills of lading (BL) and will have the term CFS/CFS mentioned. This means that the shipping line's responsibility begins at the CFS (Container Freight Station) in port of loading and ends at the CFS in port of discharge. The freight for these are charged by the line directly to the shippers in proportion to the amount of cargo they have received from the shipper.

[In modern times, incidences of shipping lines acting as a consolidator are few and far between. A groupage operator or consolidator – defined next – acts in its stead.]

8.4   FCL AND LCL - DIFFERENCE IN TRANSIT TIME

It is not unusual for an LCL shipment to take more time in transit than a FCL shipment from the same departure port designated for the same destination. It happens because in the case of a FCL shipment, the container carries cargo from a single shipper to a single consignee. Once it is packed at the port of loading, it is not reworked anywhere. Except for being re-handled or re-directed at a transhipment port (in case there is no direct service from point to point), it is delivered 'as is' to the port of discharge or delivery.

In the case of LCL (or groupage) cargo, the shipping line or groupage operator loads in the same container cargoes belonging to many shippers and many consignees, and convert it to an FCL container for the carrier touching various ports in the general direction of the cargo vessel's route.

It is important to clearly understand that an LCL container may be de-consolidated and re-consolidated in transit as explained below (a probable cause for longer transit time and greater risk compared to a FCL container):

"... the expression LCL merely indicates that the seller's goods have been packed into a consolidated or FAK (freight all kinds) container with other shippers' goods. It need not even be that all these shipments are going to the same destination. For example, if a shipper has 4cbm of cargo for, say, Chittagong, it will be consolidated into a container by a consolidator or groupage operator (who is unknown to the shipper as it is their shipper's forwarder who arranges this) and sent to the consolidator's agent at a hub like Singapore. There, that container will be unpacked (de-consolidated), put aside temporarily and then consolidated with other LCL cargo coming from other origins destined for Chittagong. Shipments involving more than one re-consolidation is also possible because of the more unusual destinations not easily serviced by the one re-consolidation." (Bob Ronai)[52]

8.5   GROUPAGE OPERATOR, CONSOLIDATOR

It is not that all countries or all shipping lines in all countries offer LCL services. In South Africa, for example, there is no concept of LCL containers. Such LCL shipments are, therefore, handled by groupage operators or "consolidators" and shipped on a FCL basis.

The groupage operator books the container with the shipping line as their own cargo. Once the cargo is consolidated and packed into a container, the consolidator (groupage operator) issue their own House Bills of Lading (HBL) to their clients (shippers) and collect the Master Bill of Lading (MBL) from the shipping line for the container which is booked with the line as an FCL, and which will show the groupage operator as a shipper on the shipping line's bill of lading (B/L).

---

[52] Bob Ronai (CDCS) was a member of the ICC Incoterms Drafting Group, and is a veteran in the field of Trade Finance. His reference to re-consolidation en route for LCL cargo shipment finds an echo in the Indian Customs Manual 2018 issued by the Indian Central Board of Indirect Taxes & Customs (updated till 31.12.2018), extracts from which are reproduced at the end of this book.

Depending on the contract with their customers the House Bill of Lading maybe termed as CFS/CFS or Door to Door. The consolidator's responsibility and delivery terms will depend on these terms mentioned on the bill of lading.

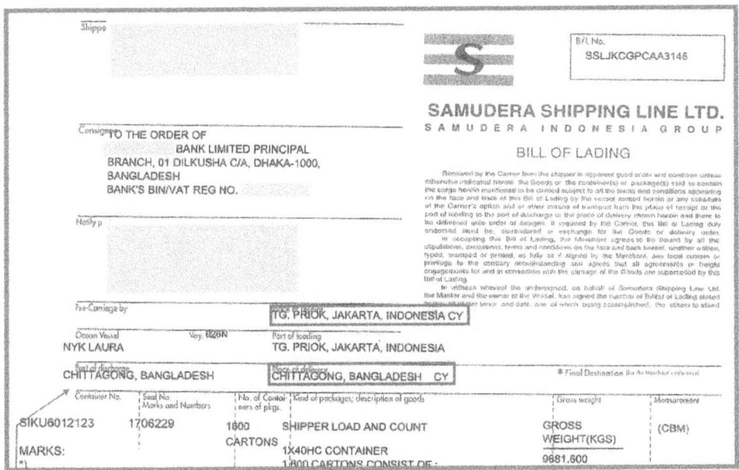

8.6   CONTAINER DELIVERY TERMS

As we may have been observed, certain terms and expressions related to container shipment have become industry standard and are used worldwide (even though not uniformly interpreted from one country to another). The precise meaning of these terms must be understood by us if justice is to be done to the trade finance operations or to transactions related to the container transport business.

The terms discussed here are CY/CY (read as CY to CY, or container yard to container yard), CFS/CFS, CFS/CY and CY/CFS. Strictly speaking, these expressions or symbols on a B/L address *routing issues* indicating terminal to terminal shipment. The terms indicate the port of origin (the starting point) and the destination (point of termination) of a particular shipment, and nothing more. Call them 'container delivery terms' if you like. The full implications of these terms are explained next.

8.7   THE DELIVERY TERMS

8.7.1   CY/CY

'CY/CY' simply means 'Container Yard to Container Yard'. If shown on the transport document, the first named CY is the departure port where the shipper delivers the fully packed and ready cargo container in a loaded and sealed condition – regardless of the quantity or weight or volume of the goods loaded into it. The second named port is the Container Yard at the *destination* port, where the shipping line will deliver that very same container in a sealed condition to the consignee. The carrier's liability starts at the container yard (CY) of the port of origin where it takes charge of the container, and ends at the CY of the destination port.

A CY, as has been explained earlier, is merely a transit point for containers hosting inbound, outbound and empties. Apart from the empties, only fully-packed and sealed containers are handled by a CY. A container must, therefore, be packed at the shipper's or the forwarder's premises prior to being received by the carrier at the CY for onward carriage to the destination CY. At the destination port, it is up to the consignee or an authorised agent to take charge of the container after the payment of port charges and duties.

By declaring CY/CY term on the bill of lading, the carrier certifies that the stuffing and de-stuffing of the container are the responsibilities of the shipper or the consignee (depending on the Incoterms mutually agreed upon by the parties). All responsibilities related to wrong stowage of the container belong to the shipper or the consignee, as the case may be.

[If a letter of credit requires a B/L to certify or state that it is a FCL shipment, it is not enough for the B/L to show that it represents a CY/CY shipment. Such an endorsement will not meet the requirement of the LC and will be deemed a discrepancy. Because, for all we know, and as has been explained a little earlier, an FCL may have been stuffed and packed by a groupage operator and effectively is an LCL container.]

8.7.2 CFS/CFS

The letters CFS/CFS (read as 'CFS to CFS') mean 'Container Freight Station to Container Freight Station'. The symbol CFS/CFS displayed on a transport document conveys the information that the container is scheduled to move from the originating CFS to a destination CFS. The letters CFS/CFS point towards the kind of shipment where loose cargo is delivered at the outbound CFS (container freight station) for grouping (consolidating) them together for a specific destination. (The container may be de-stuffed and again re-stuffed somewhere along the way.)

The goods are delivered at the destination CFS where they are de-consolidated. After customs clearance and payment of port charges, the consignees receive and arrange for the delivery of the loose cargo from the container freight station for onward transportation to their final destination or place or use. A shipping line's responsibility begins at the CFS (Container Freight Station) at the port of loading and ends at the CFS at the port of discharge.

8.7.3   CFS/CY

Literally translated, the letters CFS/CY indicate the fact that the shipment is meant to begin at a departing Container Freight Station (CFS) and terminate at the destination Container Yard (CY). The cargo from multiple consignors is consolidated or grouped together at a CFS at origin port. However at the destination, the delivery of the container takes place at a Container Yard, for being further transported by the single consignee to his/her place of choice at their risk and responsibility.

This manner of transportation usually indicates a buyer-consolidation shipment. Such shipments usually have multiple shippers/sellers but a single consignee/buyer. (Scenario: multiple sellers > single buyer.)

8.7.4   CY/CFS

When cargo is received at a Container Yard (CY) at the port of origin but delivered to a Container Freight Station (CFS) at the destination port for the purpose of de-consolidation (the consignees are assumed to be more than one), the term mentioned on the B/L is CY/CFS.

Under this arrangement the container is packed at the shipper's or the forwarder's premises, locked, sealed and customs cleared before delivery to the carrier at the Container Yard (CY). That same container is de-consolidated at the carrier's container freight station (CFS) at the destination port prior to the consignments being handed over to their respective consignees. The respective consignees arrange the delivery of the loose cargo from the container freight station to their respective final destinations. (Scenario: single seller > multiple buyers.)

8.8   KEY TAKEAWAYS:

a. Every *container* BL is in fact a multimodal transport document, because the carrier takes charge of the goods at a CY or CFS somewhere inland. The nature of the document is revealed by way of notations on the document itself – such as FCL/FCL, LCL/LCL, CFS/CFS or CY/CY.

b. More often than not, for various reasons (including congestion, higher charges nearer to the port areas) a CFS is located slightly away from a port (but not as far as an ICD might be). Goods are stuffed or de-stuffed at a CFS, not at a CY. Therefore, goods have to travel a larger distance when booked on CFS/CFS terms.

c. For port-to-port shipments the carrier will either issue CY or CFS terms depending on whether the cargo is FCL or LCL.

CY/CY and CY/CFS are port-to-port shipments. Door-to-door shipments are those where the carrier is responsible for the entire stretch of the movement – from pickup to delivery.

d. The 'haulage'[53] of the container to the terminal is almost never carried out by the shipper themselves. There is always a haulage company involved whether contracted for the job by the forwarder or the packer. They are the experts. The forwarder – in turn – may have been appointed by the overseas buyer or the local seller, depending on the terms in the contract and the ICC Incoterms rule used.

e. It is not necessary for a shipper or consignee of a 'less than container load' (LCL) shipment to know which ship the cargo is going on board. But the information is available, if necessary.

f. In practice, the freight charged does not cover/include the haulage by truck from the seller's premises to the CY in port of loading or the haulage by truck from the CY in port of discharge to the buyer's premises. Hence the seller will usually use a forwarder to arrange truck haulage to the CY in port of loading, and the buyer (or, the seller – based on the contract and the Incoterms rule chosen) will use a forwarder or customs clearing agent to arrange truck haulage from CY at the port of discharge to a place nominated by the buyer or the consignee. (Caution: Check the Incoterms rule used.)

---

[53] See section 12.1.1 for more information.

g. Following from the above, it is the responsibility of either the shipper or the consignee to arrange for transportation of the cargo to the Container Yard/Container Freight Station (CY/CFS) for outgoing cargo, or to take delivery from the Container Yard/Container Freight Station (CY/CFS) at the destination port for incoming cargo.

h. A container may be stuffed and sealed at the seller's/consignor's premises under Customs supervision and delivered to a CY at the departure port for onward transportation. This will be termed as a CY/CY shipment. In contrast, for LCL shipment, the individual sellers or consignors must bring their cargo to the consolidation area for customs clearance etc. before being consolidated, packed into a container and the container sealed. The place where this consolidation takes place is a CFS.

i. To know who bears the charges for what, refer to the ICC Incoterms 2020 rules.

8.9   FCL/FCL AND OTHER TERMS EXPLAINED

A few more terms related to container shipment are explained below in brief. It must be reiterated that the terms do not have any direct bearing on the movement of the container shipment, the port of origin or destination. Instead, these terms describe, however pithily, issues related to the consignor, consignee, consolidation of goods and so on. The inference to the nature of the origin or the destination port is only incidental to the main issues under discussion, which would become clear as we go along. Let us now look at the terms more closely.

FCL/FCL: This indicates that the shipment is a 'Full Container Load' at the port of origin, and the delivery at destination is also as a 'Full Container Load'. FCL/FCL usually means that the shipper is a single person (or organisation) and the consignee is similarly a single person (or organisation). The inference is that the transportation of the container(s) will take place uninterrupted from one CY and terminate at another CY, for being custom cleared and handed over to the consignee for onward carriage to destination without de-stuffing or de-consolidation anywhere in between. It is (usually, but not necessarily) a 'single seller and single buyer' scenario. This mode is faster and cost-effective. Since the shipment originates at a CY and terminates at a CY, an FCL/FCL shipment is also described as a CY/CY shipment.

FCL/LCL: This term indicates that the shipment is a 'Full Container Load' *at the port of origin* (pointing towards a single seller). But the goods in the container are meant for more than one buyer or consignor. Hence the shipment must arrive only at a CFS – not at a CY – because only at the CFS can a container be de-consolidated and the goods delivered to the various consignees. The respective consignees are expected to custom-clear, pay the port dues and receive the goods for onward transportation by their own carriage at their risk and cost to the final destination. Since the shipment originates at a CY but terminates at a CFS, an FCL/LCL shipment is also described as a CY/CFS shipment.

LCL/LCL: This represents a 'Less than a Container Load to Less than a Container Load' shipment. This term does not have any bearing on whether the container is half-empty or more than half-full. The term LCL/LCL is applied to indicate the fact that the container is stuffed with goods being despatched by more than a single shipper, and are meant for more than a single (i.e. multiple) consignee/buyer.

It's a 'multiple-seller/multiple-buyer' scenario, the goods being consolidated at the port of origin before delivery to the CFS. The shipment will also be delivered only to a CFS for de-stuffing (de-consolidation) and delivery to the respective consignees. Since the shipment originates at a CFS and terminates also at a CFS, the expression CFS/CFS is used to describe a LCL/LCL shipment.

LCL/FCL: This symbol goes on to indicate that the container was stuffed with goods shipped by more than a single consignor. But that the goods are consigned to (are meant for) a single consignee or a single buyer. Since it is a LCL (outward) shipment, the outbound goods must be consolidated and stuffed – which can be done only at a Container Freight Station (CFS), not at a Container Yard (CY). However, since the shipment is meant for a single buyer/consignor, the delivery of the container to the consignee would be made at a CY. After customs clearance and payment of port duties and charges, the consignee will take delivery of the container, cart it away to a place of his choice for de-stuffing.

This is a 'multiple seller-single buyer' scenario, and is consequently referred to in terms of the origin/destination ports as a CFS/CY shipment.

8.10   CONSOLIDATION OF CARGO (Indian context)

[Extracts from Chapter 11, page 99 of the Indian Customs Manual 2018 issued by the Central Board of Indirect Taxes & Customs (Updated till 31.12.2018. It refers to an interesting aspect of LCL shipment not known to many.)]

"1. Introduction:

1.1   With the development of a number of ICDs/CFSs in the hinterland, importers and exporters have the option to either get their import/export consignments cleared at the gateway ports or any nearby ICD/CFS. The export goods cleared by Customs at an ICD/CFS are sent in sealed containers to gateway port where these containers are normally allowed to be exported without further examination of the goods. Similarly, imported cargo meant for any ICD/CFS is allowed to be transhipped in sealed containers from the gateway ports to such ICDs/CFSs and all Customs formalities in relation to clearance of cargo are completed by the importers at ICD/CFS.

1.2   Export containers sealed at the ICD/CFS were earlier not allowed to be re-opened for consolidation at the gateway port, which led to shifting this activity to international hub ports e.g. Dubai, Singapore and Colombo. Similarly, import containers with LCL cargoes used to be brought to hub ports, where shipping lines used to consolidate the cargo and stuff in containers destination wise. There was thus a demand from exporters, importers, shipping lines, agents and consolidators to allow the reworking of containers at the gateway ports to avoid the extra expenditure incurred for undertaking the same job at the foreign hub ports.

1.3   The facility of re-working containers is now allowed at the gateway ports. Shipping lines can take containers stuffed with LCL export cargo, irrespective of destination, from ICD/CFS to a gateway port, where these can be opened and re-worked with cargo received from different ICDs/CFSs and stuffed in containers, destination-wise. Similarly, LCL import cargo brought at any gateway port can be re-worked and consolidated in containers ICD-wise. With this facility, the exporters get benefited by saving in freight charges, reduction in transit time, better handling and safer delivery of cargo as the activity takes place under the supervision of Indian agencies.

The facility also reduces freight charges for imported LCL cargo as it helps in optimum utilization of container capacity.

It also helps in attracting business for Indian ports and developing them as transhipment hubs."

The following procedures are also outlined in the same section of the Manual:

- Rules and procedure for consolidation of import cargo:

- Rules and procedure for consolidation of export cargo

- Rules and procedure for international transhipment of LCL containers at Indian ports.

CHAPTER 9

CONTAINER TRANSPORT DOCUMENTS

9.1   BILLS OF LADING (B/L)

We referred to a house bill of lading (HBL) and a master bill of lading (MBL) in the previous chapter. An understanding of the difference between a house bill of lading (HBL) and a master bill of lading (MBL) is important if we are to clearly understand the inter-relationships among the shipper, the consolidator, the freight forwarder or a NVOCC operator, and the liner that carries the container to its destination.

9.2   HOUSE BILL OF LADING

The house bill of lading (HBL) is issued by an NVOCC operator or a freight forwarder to the shipper and is:

- *A receipt of goods shipped.* So when the HBL is issued, the cargo has actually been loaded onto a ship

- *A document of title.* While it is not completely negotiable, it does serve the same purpose as a normal carrier bill of lading and must be surrendered in original by the importer to the freight forwarder at destination in order to receive the cargo. (Refer to UCP 600 article 20 for more information on the characteristics of an ocean B/L.)

- *Proof of contract of carriage* between the customer and the freight forwarder.

When issued for a FCL shipment (non-groupage), a HBL should always be issued on the back of a MBL, meaning that the HBL should be an *exact* replica of the MBL issued by the actual shipping line in respect of all details except for the details about the shipper, the consignee and the notify party. These details will be different in the HBL and MBL.

The house bill of lading (HBL) issued by the freight forwarder might state the vessel and voyage the cargo is intended to load on. That would refer only to the first leg and is not necessarily the vessel that would be carrying the cargo all the way to its destination port.

The house bill of lading has details of the actual shipper and consignee, the cargo being shipped, payment terms and contact details of the forwarder or their agent. The shipper need to send the original house bill of lading to the consignee. The consignee need to hand the original house bill of lading to the freight forwarder at destination in order to take delivery of the goods.

9.3   MASTER BILL OF LADING

The master bill of lading (or carrier B/L) is issued by the shipping line to the NVOCC operator or the freight forwarder when the container with multiple shipments has been loaded onto a ship. It is not relevant for the shipper or consignee of the less than container load (LCL) shipment, as they would refer to the house bill of lading that relates directly to their shipment.

In the MBL,

♦ the shipper will usually be the NVOCC operator, or their agent or the freight forwarder;

♦ the consignee will usually be the destination agent or counterpart or office of the NVOCC operator, or the freight forwarder;

♦ the 'Notify Party' could be the same as the consignee or any other party.

It is the freight forwarder's decision which shipping line, origin and destination ports to use. This is, in principle, irrelevant to the LCL shipper or the consignee, as the shipment will always pass through an origin and destination warehouse.

9.4   SEA WAYBILL

A sea waybill has many similarities with the house bill of lading, but does not require an original to be surrendered to the freight forwarder before the cargo can be handed over to the consignee. It is not a negotiable document and is not a document of title.

9.5   MULTIMODAL TRANSPORT DOCUMENT

It is a document issued or signed by a carrier indicating carriage by more than one means of transportation. For example, a multimodal transport document for a door-to-port shipment with main carriage by a sea-going vessel might indicate pickup at the place where the shipment originates (often the seller´s premises inland) with pre-carriage by truck and main carriage from the named port of loading to the named port of discharge by a named vessel.

Depending on how the contact of carriage was drafted, the document could be issued either on a 'received for shipment' basis at any time after the goods entered the control of the main carrier, or on an 'on-board' basis after the goods were loaded in the named vessel.

> "Whilst a transport document covering a multimodal or combined shipment may take the form of a Bill of Lading, Road Waybill, Rail Waybill or an Inland Waterway Transport Document, traders and bankers should be aware of the differences between them. A bill of lading for a multimodal transport shipment can be a document of title, while a land carriage document is not such a document. ... Whether a transport document is a Port-to-Port or a Multimodal Transport Bill of Lading depends on the type of service required as particularized on the face of the document. Bankers should check what notations contain the Bills of

Lading in respect of places of receipt and delivery, as well as the vessel's name, shipment date and freight.

Bills of Lading for container shipments commonly show a place of receipt and a place of delivery in addition to ports of loading and discharge. When these places of receipt and delivery are the same as the stated ports of loading and discharge, e.g. as is the case with Container Yards and Container Freight Stations, the Bill of Lading indicates a port-to-port shipment. When they are different in the sense that either one or both of these places are situated inland, then the Bill of Lading evidences a multimodal transport.

The issue with UCP 600 article 19 (Transport document covering at least two different modes of transport) is not what type of documents to ask for but to use proper wording in L/C. ... The multimodal transport document does not have to bear one name or another but must fulfil the requirements set in UCP 600 article 19. A liner Bill of Lading or a CMR Consignment Note may cover a multimodal transport shipment, or the same document may be used for uni-modal carriage only. It all depends on the information shown on the transport document and the wording of the L/C." [54]

In spite of the foregoing, this writer continued to harbour certain confusions with regard to the nature of B/Ls issued. So a few

---

[54] *Multimodal transport documents and the UCP 600 - Frequently asked questions on the MMTD document*, Kim Sindberg
https://www.lcviews.com/index.php?page_id=18

questions were put to Robert (Bob) Ronai, an expert on the subject.

The questions were as follows:

> "A groupage operator may consolidate the cargo, lock up the container and issue its own HBL to the respective shippers. Let's assume that there are multiple sellers but only one buyer. When it submits the container to the carrier for shipment to destination, (a) Does it move through a CY before arriving at the port for loading? (b) Presumably it makes no difference to the carrier whether it was a FCL or LCL shipment since it receives a locked and sealed container. The carrier may, therefore, issue its B/L that shows CY/CY on the B/L. Correct? Therefore, who declares to the carrier whether it's LCL or FCL (for insertion on a B/L)?"

Bob Ronai responded as follows:

> For a groupage container all cargo is received loose into the container freight station (CFS) of that groupage operator. The possibilities now diverge – who contracted the groupage operator? In the above scenario it would usually be the buyer. So each seller will be given a groupage operator's house B/L showing LCL/FCL or CFS/CY. The groupage operator separately has booked that full container with the shipping line who will issue its master B/L (MBL) showing FCL/FCL or CY/CY and the groupage operator as shipper and the operator's destination agent as consignee – this may well actually be a sea waybill or express release B/L.

One of the reasons for the difference is where and how the groupage operator receives the cargo and takes on the contract of carriage vs. where the shipping line takes on the next contract of carriage for the full container received at its terminal (CY).

Further:

A B/L marked by a carrier as CY/CY means that they received a sealed full container (FCL) typically packed by the seller at their own premises, into their container yard (CY) in the origin country, and have contracted to deliver that sealed FCL at a CY in the destination country, from which the buyer will take it to their premises to unpack. The carrier has no direct knowledge of what is in the container. It is unusual these days for a carrier to show "FCL/FCL"; this was something dreamed up by the applicant or issuing bank in the case referred to in the ICC BC Opinion[55]. So CY/CY = FCL/FCL.

In the case of LCL cargo, there is another party involved. The seller's cargo is taken loose to a groupage operator or consolidator's premises (CFS = container freight station). There that cargo along with other shipper's cargoes, for usually other buyer's cargoes at (to) the same destination, will be consolidated or grouped into a full container.

Let's now add another complication. What the seller, buyer and bankers don't see is that sometimes that FCL ends up in

---

[55] *ICC Opinion R810 / TA817rev*

a transhipment port. For example, the seller in Sydney has two pallets for a buyer in Phnom Penh, but the consolidator has no other cargoes for that destination. Therefore that cargo will be put in an FCL with other cargoes for various places in that region and sent to the consolidator's agent in Singapore. *There the FCL is unpacked or deconsolidated*, and the cargo for Phnom Penh will be consolidated with other cargo that the consolidator in Singapore will receive similarly from elsewhere around the world and sent to Phnom Penh.[56]

The worst experienced was a shipment of 6cbm of machinery from Sydney to Lagos. The consolidator sent it to their agent in Durban, who had no other cargo expected in for Lagos so sent it in a consolidation to Rotterdam. There it was combined with other cargo for Lagos and got there six months after shipment from Sydney. It happened!

Back to the stated scenario: For a buyer to be able to consolidate its LCL purchases into one container it will do so on FCA, collecting cargo from the seller's premises or having sellers deliver their cargo to the CFS. There they will be consolidated into the one container. The consolidator will issue individual HBLs to each seller showing the seller as shipper and the buyer as consignee, each marked CFS/CY.

---

[56] A reason for delays in transit – even for FCL shipment. Hence the need for chartered vessels to ensure faster delivery and to avoid possible theft or damage to the goods during deconsolidation and reconsolidation.

That sealed container is then delivered from the CFS into the shipping company's terminal as a CY. The shipping company has no idea who the individual shippers are, the shipper on the B/L for the FCL would usually be the consolidator. In this case the consignee is the buyer who will receive the sealed FCL at the destination CY and take it to their premises to unpack. This B/L will be marked CY/CY as explained in my first paragraph.

So it all depends where you are standing while viewing the transport chain.

The above goes to underscore the fact that one must have a good grasp of the basics of container shipment and the terminologies associated with it, in order to understand the mechanism of container transportation and the Incoterms 2020 rules in their entirety.

9.6   CONTAINERISED CARGO: 'SAID TO CONTAIN'

In the case of containerised cargo, especially FCL cargo, the carrier/agents are not privy to the nature of the cargo, the loading or the packing of the containers as these operations are carried out by the client on their premises or at the CFS. Normally, the carrier or its agent is not present at the time of loading or packing. The carrier, therefore, must necessarily rely on the information (declaration) provided by the shipper in terms of the cargo, number of packages, weight, measurement and so on for issuing a B/L to the shipper.

Since the carriers or their agents do not know (plus, unable to ascertain to their own satisfaction) the condition of the cargo inside a container, they are not willing to accept liability for the same.

For this reason the shipping lines refuse to add the word 'clean' on such transport documents.

Instead, to protect themselves from any claim that the shipper might place on them at a later stage, endorsements such as, "shippers load, stow and count" or "said to contain" are seen on the transport documents (refer to UCP sub-article 26.b).

This means the shipping line is stating that they don't know the nature of the cargo, the quantity or their weight inside the container and they are accepting the shipper's declaration of the goods under the 'Said to Contain' endorsement.

In the case of bulk and break bulk shipments, this clause is not shown because the carrier can clearly see what, how many or how much they are receiving and in what condition.

It is important that the buyers and the banks issuing documentary credits (issuing banks) understand these points related to container shipment and act accordingly.

CHAPTER 10

LOADING AND UNLOADING OPERATIONS

10.1   CONTAINERS LOST AT SEA

According to the World Shipping Council (WSC), in 2023 out of the 250 million containers transported a record low of 221 were lost at sea. This is the lowest number since the survey began in 2008. The previous lowest ever loss was 661 containers lost in 2022.

Apart from the weather conditions (beyond human control) the other reasons were (a) human error, (b) human negligence, and (c) structural issues (also being under human control).

Maritime Professionals[57] says that "…there might have been several causes. This included stormy weather, ship design,

---

[57]   https://maritime-professionals.com/why-are-shipping-containers-lost-at-sea-and-where-do-they-end-up/

propulsion issues and how containers are lashed together including varying regulations around the latter. The degradation of containers and resulting metal fatigue also contribute. In some instances, containers may not be loaded correctly and inadequately secured for rough seas."[58]

The primary reasons were attributed to the following:

a) Improper stowage and securing,

b) Incorrectly (fraudulently?) declared weight of containers,

c) Poor packing or stowage leading to shifting of cargo inside a container, consequent instability,

d) Taking on loads that are much larger and higher, thus compromising on overall stability, especially in bad weather,

e) Shortcuts to save costs by reducing expenditure on securing components, lashing materials or overloading,

f) Structural failures in terms of damaged or weak containers, inadequate lashing equipment and so on,

g) Insufficient maintenance, lack of lashing and blocking components,

h) Metal fatigue – linked to poor maintenance,

i) Parametric rolling,

---

[58]   https://maritime-professionals.com/why-are-shipping-containers-lost-at-sea-and-where-do-they-end-up/

j)   The effects of climate change.

It is not that there is always a single contributory factor leading to a disaster. Faults and flaws – minor or not so minor – may add up leading to a bigger disaster.

Some of the terms used above are explained in the pages that follow. Their importance will be understood and appreciated in the light of the incidence of loss described above.

10.2   CONSOLIDATION, GROUPAGE OPERATION

The terms "groupage" and "groupage operator" were mentioned several times in the preceding pages, and its function explained in section 8.5.

The term "consolidation" is defined as the act of collecting the LCL cargo from the various shippers and packing them into a single container – properly stuffed and stacked – to make up a full container load (FCL). The entities that handle such operations are known as *Consolidators* or *Groupage Operators*.

It is useful to note that in case of consolidation cargo, the consolidators issue their House Bills of Lading (HBL) to the shippers, and secure a Master Bill of Lading from the shipping line (or simply 'line') for the container which is booked with the line as an FCL and which will show them (the consolidator) as a shipper on the line's bill of lading.

10.3 STUFFING

Stuffing (in marine transport) is the process of loading of cargo into freight containers or other mode of transport. To "stow" is to place or arrange compactly and put safely in place. This is a traditional seafaring word. The International Maritime Organization refers to that operation as "packing". The container is then sealed (often in the presence of Customs), and transported to the carrier for loading on board a vessel and onward carriage to destination.

10.4 DE-STUFFING

In marine transport, de-stuffing, stripping or devanning is the reverse of stuffing. When the cargo has reached its destination and has passed the customs clearance process, it has to be de-stuffed. It's the process of unloading of various (small) consignments from a single container. This is where products are inspected for damage, catalogued and unloaded by personnel.

10.5   STUFFING A CONTAINER[59]

Shipping line negotiates freight terms, etc. with the client and upon finalization of deal; client agrees to use 'X' for export shipment. The client then approaches the shipping line operations office/counter at the ICD for the allotment of the container. Container is allotted to the client upon the presentation of a copy of shipping bill/invoice. The options for loading and packing of a container are as follows:

10.5.1 Factory stuffing

If the container is being taken to the factory for stuffing, the client organizes his own transportation and removes the container for house stuffing. After stuffing, the central excise puts a seal in the container and Line seal is also put by the shipper. The container is moved to ICD (as applicable), where a customs inspection takes place, and after inspection Customs seal is put. After the sealing, the container moves to the railhead for further movement to the departure port.

10.5.2 ICD stuffing

The cargo is brought to the ICD by the shipper and a container is allowed based on shipping bill a container is allotted. Cargo is stuffed at ICD and after the seals are put in the container, the container moves to the railhead for further movement to the departure port.

---

[59]   https://www.ukessays.com/essays/economics/export-cycle-of-a-shipping-line-economics-essay.php

10.5.3 CFS stuffing

The cargo is brought to the CFS by the shipper. After the customs formalities, the container is stuffed by the shipping line or the groupage operator. After stuffing, a line seal and customs seal are put, and the container is moved to ICD railhead for further movement to the loadport.

Many a times the shipper stuffs the container in his factory and instead of bringing it back to the ICD, hands it over directly to the loadport. Customs inspection of seal is done at the loadport.

10.6 STRAPPING

An operation by which supply containers, such as cartons or boxes, are reinforced by bands, metal straps, or wire, placed at specified intervals around them, drawn taut, and then sealed or clamped by a machine.

10.7 STOWAGE

Stowage is defined as the proper arrangement in a ship, of the different articles of which a cargo consists, so that they may not injure each other by friction, or be damaged by the leakage of the ship. Stowage also means the proper placement of dangerous goods on board a ship in order to ensure safety and environmental protection during transport. Stowage requirements are different for container ships, ro-ro ships, general cargo ships and barge-carrying ships.

10.8   STOWAGE PLANNING

In a sea voyage stowage planning is a critical and complex operation for containers. The carrier and port operators have vessel planners who plan safe stowage of containers. This planning is done to avoid container shifting, and to ensure that safety initiatives are carried out – especially when the weight of each container is different, as this can affect vessel rolling during voyage.

Each container has a different gross weight which is only known once the container is delivered into the CY. Since container ships discharge containers destined for a particular port and may load more containers from that port, container ships often have to reposition (unload/reload) containers at each port in order to maintain balance.

A container vessel in one voyage calls at multiple ports, a break bulk vessel likely calls at fewer ports and does not typically stow one lot of cargo on top of another. If well planned, a CY/CY shipment may call at very few ports in between its departure point and destination port.

10.9   TRIPPING

Stripping or devanning is the unloading of various small consignments from a single container, or the removal of goods from a standard container to the warehouse or to an open ground for the client to load out.

10.10 DEVANNING

Devanning in simple terms is the act of removing cargo from a previously sealed container. It is also commonly known as the stripping, unstuffing, de-stuffing or unloading of the container. Typically, full container load (FCL) shipments are devanned at the destination warehouse. Less-than container load (LCL) shipments are devanned at the destination Container Freight Station (CFS). This is process is also sometimes called "de-consolidation".

10.11 CARGO LASHING AND SECURING[60]

If the storage of cargo is not properly stowed or is not secure enough then there is no escape from the vagaries of the weather. This may take a toll on the loaded cargo, causing damage to other cargo in the vicinity or to the vessel's structures and fittings and even throwing the cargo overboard. Improper cargo lashing and failure to adhere to the procedures required for cargo stowage on ships is dangerous to property, life and environment at sea. The extremely necessary process calls for a lot of skill and expertise.

10.12 TRIMMING (LOADING CARGO)

It is defined as the partial or total levelling of the cargo within the holds by means of loading spouts or chutes, portable machinery or manually. It means the adding, removal or shifting of weight in a ship to achieve the required forward and aft draughts.

---

[60] https://www.marineinsight.com/marine-safety/the-basics-of-lashing-and-cargo-securing-on-ships/

10.13 SEGREGATION

Segregation is the process of separating two or more substances or articles which are considered mutually incompatible when their packing or stowage together may result in undue hazards in case of leakage or spillage, or any other accident. Segregation is obtained by maintaining certain distances between incompatible, dangerous goods or by requiring the presence of one or more steel bulkheads or decks between them, or a combination thereof.

10.14 DE-CONSOLIDATION

De-consolidation is the opposite of 'consolidation'. De-consolidation is the process of unloading and segregating the contents of a single container among the consignees designated by the original shippers. Handing over the consignments to the respective consignees is subject to custom clearance and other port formalities.

10.15 DUNNAGE[61]

It is the name for the materials used in holds and containers to protect goods and their packaging from moisture, contamination and mechanical damage. Dunnage may include plastic films, jute coverings, tarpaulins, wood (wooden dunnage), rice matting, nonwovens, liner bags or also inlets etc. Depending on the use to which it is put, dunnage may be divided into floor, lateral, interlayer and top dunnage.

---

[61] https://www.tis-gdv.de/tis_e/misc/garnier-htm/

10.16 SHIPPER'S LOAD, STOW AND COUNT

In containerized shipping, a carrier often do not – rather cannot – physically inspect the goods within a container, In order to avoid liability or claim on account of the cargo they carry, a carrier may add clauses like "Shipper's Load, Stow and Count" (SLAC) or "Said to Contain" (STC) to protect themselves from claims related to the contents of the container.

Shipper's Load, Stow and Count thus refers to the condition that:

- *the shipper has loaded* the goods into the container using their own means/methods of loading;

- *the shipper has stowed* the goods *loaded* in the container in a manner safe for transport. This also means that the shipper may be liable for cargo damage due to improper stowage of cargo in the container.

- *the shipper has counted* the goods loaded and stowed in the container.

What the *Shipper's Load, Stow and Count* clause doesn't say is about the nature of the goods. This is covered under the 'Said to Contain' (STC) endorsement.

CHAPTER 11

EXPRESSIONS AND CHARGES RELATED TO CONTAINER MOVEMENT

11.1　STORAGE

The word 'storage' when used in the context of maritime shipping, connotes a meaning that is altogether different from its usual application in the English language. All ports offer a certain free period to allow the customer time to comply with, process import requirements and take delivery of the containers from the port. After this free period charges (also known as port storage) will apply. This charge, included in the rates of the carrier, is levied by the port or the terminal to the shipping line, which in turn will then bill the customer. In some countries it is billed directly to the customer by the port.

More information on port charges appear at section 11.12.

11.2 DEMURRAGE & DETENTION - INTRODUCTION[62]

The journey of a container does not end with its arrival at its destination or its point of delivery of the goods inside. The customer must clean it and return it to an agreed location, such as the port or a container terminal or depot, within a pre-arranged period of time so that it can be re-used for another shipment. In order for millions of containers to continuously move around the world, it's important that carriers can keep equipment available and ready to move at all time.

Demurrage and detention are penal charges, incurred if the user of the container exceeds the 'free time' offered by carriers. For example, if the consignee's full container is waiting too long at the arrival port before being picked up and gated out at the destination terminal, or if the consignee takes too long to release and return the empty container to the port or a pre-arranged destination, penal charges are levied.

A worked out example as to how demurrage, detention and port charges are levied is available as annexure 01.

11.3 DEMURRAGE

Demurrage relates to container or cargo while it stays in the port area beyond the 'free time' allowed for/when loading (exports) or unloading (imports). Demurrage is measured from when a container is offloaded from the carrying vessel or the railway (as the case may be) until it is picked up at the port for its onward

---

[62] Refer to annexure I for a worked out example.

journey. If cargo operations are not finished before the 'lay time' (see 11.7) expires, the charterer is in breach and must pay penal charges known as demurrage. The charge is levied by the shipping line to the importer. The demurrage rate is agreed in advance as a term of the charter-party and is usually a fixed amount per day (or pro rata for part of a day).

Demurrage chargeable time = Dwell Time – Free Time (if dwell time *exceeds* free time).

It is imperative to ensure that, before executing the contract of carriage, both parties are clear on the lay time and, most importantly, on clauses which stipulate where a charterer is relieved of its obligation to pay demurrage or where the rate payable is reduced by half. Failure to do so could prove costly.

11.4   DESPATCH

The inverse of 'demurrage' is 'despatch' and paid out as a bonus. If the cargo operations are finished by the charterer before the lay time expires, then the voyage will be more profitable for the owner, as the cycle will be completed more quickly. In these circumstances, it is common for the owner to offer both an incentive and a reward for quick cargo operations. The sum the owner agrees to pay to the charterer is called *'despatch',* a bonus for efficient cargo operation. This, too, is usually agreed as a term of the charter-party at (possibly) half the demurrage rate. But this also depends on the terms of the charter party.

Despatch is most common in dry cargo shipping, and is normally not included in charter parties in the tanker or gas segments.

11.5   DETENTION

'Demurrage' and 'detention' are both penalties for delays. The difference will be easy to remember if you note that 'demurrage' is incurred when the container is *inside* the port/terminal area, and 'detention' charges are incurred when the container is *outside* the port/terminal area.

Detention relates to a container that is empty after unpacking or before re-packing. Detention is defined as the period *beyond* the (free) time allowed to the importer from gate-out, to unload the container *and return it to the nominated depot*. Where the empty container is not returned to the nominated depot within the agreed free-time, detention charges are incurred.

So basically, before the full container is picked up, 'demurrage' may be charged (after expiry of free days). After the container has been picked up, till the time the empty is returned to the lines-nominated depot, 'detention' may be charged for 'delays'. The most common market practice is to combine demurrage and detention. But there are instances where these are charged separately.

In the case of exports, normally lines give a few free days within which the shipper (or a forwarder) has to pick up the empty, pack it and return it full to the port. In case of delays for more than what the free period allows, the line charges 'detention' for the days that the empty is kept with the client as empty or full.

Once the container is packed, but the shipper is unable to ship the same due to any reason whatsoever, then 'demurrage' will be levied at the rate fixed by the line till the full container is shipped out.

The extent of free time or details regarding nomenclature, and also that of 'storage', is likely to vary from country to country or port to port.

Demurrage and detention do not apply to LCL shipments (the consolidation being carried out by the lines themselves). These are applicable only for FCL shipments or where the shipment is handled by a consolidator (groupage operator).

11.6   FREE TIME

If a container is not working (earning) for its owner, that resource is being wasted. It is like cash in a bank's locker – non-remunerative, idle cash. Lay time, free time and dwell time are terms related to container shipment, more specifically to its movement or the lack of it. It must be clarified that 'free time' and 'dwell time' are applied in relation to containers.

Free time, or standard free time, is related to *container* movement. It is defined as the period of time that a carrier gives its customers for demurrage and/or detention activities, free of charge. Also called 'port free days', it is the period during which a container can be stored at a port or terminal without incurring additional charges by way of demurrage or storage fees. Once the free time expires, the clock starts ticking and charges may be attracted.

11.7   LAY TIME[63]

Lay time relates to *vessel* movement. This is the time permitted by the port authorities for a vessel to complete loading or unloading operations at a port. It is the agreed span of time that may be taken to load and discharge the cargo carried on board the vessel without incurring extra charges (demurrage). Demurrage is compensation for failure to load or discharge the vessel within lay time. The objective is to avoid congestion at a port.

When negotiating a charter-party, the owners will calculate how much freight they require to compensate them for performing the voyage. A key factor is how long the voyage will take to perform, that is, the approach voyage (arrival), loading, the carrying voyage and discharging. An owner usually has no control over the loading and discharging, and therefore the charterer will accept an obligation to load and discharge the cargo within a fixed time called 'lay time'. It may be measured in days, hours and even tides.

The commercial purpose of lay time is, therefore, to compensate the owner for the time spent by the charterer in loading and discharging the cargo over which the owner has no control.

---

[63]   http://www.plimsollconsultancy.com/index.php/laytime-demurrage-tanker-trade/

When does lay time commence?

Before a vessel is ready to commence loading or discharging, it must be at the destination as specified in the charter-party and ready to take on or discharge cargo. Further, where required, a notice of readiness (NOR) must be issued to the charterer of the vessel, notifying him or her that the vessel is ready. Lay time typically commences after a valid NOR has been tendered. When these conditions have been fulfilled, the vessel is classed as an 'arrived ship'.

11.8   DWELL TIME

It is defined as the time a *conveyance* (bus, truck, train, or ship) is allowed to load or unload passengers or freight at a terminal without any additional charge. For freight terminals, dwell time refers to the time cargo stays in a terminal yard or storage area while waiting to be loaded. Dwell time may be operational, transactional or storage related. One of the key performance indicators of cargo terminal operations at any port or airport is the dwell time, the lower being the better.

Container Dwell Time: This refers to the total time a *container* spends at a port or terminal, from the moment it is unloaded from an incoming vessel carrying the container until it is moved out of the facility by sea, truck or by rail. It is the time a container remains at a port, terminal, or rail yard after being offloaded from a vessel or train, while waiting for paperwork, customs clearance, and other logistical processes before it can move out of the port area.

Longer dwell time increases costs. Less dwell time indicates higher efficiency. Demurrage fees are accumulated when a container exceeds the allotted free time, increasing shipping costs.

For air cargo, more or less airport dwell time equals the duration cargo is discharged and transported from freights to the hub in order to be stored until the time the goods owner has released the goods and dismissed it from terminals. Where this period exceeds the prescribed time, it is said that the cargo or goods have dwelled.[64]

11.9   GATE IN

These are terms used at various stages of the movement of containers. The delivery of the laden container into port is called 'gating in' or 'gate in'. It's the process where a full container, sealed and loaded on a transport unit (road, rail, inland waterway) is taken over by the port cargo-handler on behalf of the shipping company at the entry gate of the departure port terminal. For less-than-container-load (LCL) shipments, the suppliers deliver the

---

[64] A survey by Container xChange, in association with German maritime research consultant FraunhoferCML, suggested that despite technological advances, containers still spend a surprisingly long time empty at depots, incurring storage costs and not earning revenue. "All containers are very much in need; they still spend on average 45 days empty at depots," says the report, which surprisingly suggests that areas which suffer from shortages have higher dwell times. "Especially in regions with low container availability such as China and the US, the average is comparably high, with 61 and 66 days respectively, compared with the global average of 45 days," notes the report. (Source: Mike Wackett in *The Loadstar,* 01/12/2020).

cargo to the container freight station (CFS), where it is consolidated and delivered to the port terminal. Once a container is 'gated in' within the scheduled 'CY cut-off time', it gets delivered to a container yard within the port area. In this container yard, port cranes will stack containers and eventually load them onto the vessel they are assigned to.

A 'Gate In price' in shipping terms indicates *explicitly* that the terminal handling charge loading (THCL) is included in the freight rate.

11.10 GATE OUT[65]

Once an inbound vessel discharges the containers, these are shunted to a temporary container yard, where specialized port cranes load the containers onto the respective trailers. The trailers head towards the exit checkpoint of the terminal, where inspection of the containers and documents are first carried out. Individual ports may have their own practices.

After all the inspections are completed and payment made, the container's gate-out date and time are logged into the port's system. The trucker may then complete the 'gate out' process by picking up the container from the port yard and leaving the exit checkpoint with the laden container.

As with Gate In, a Gate Out freight rate includes the terminal handling charge (THC).

---

[65] ibid

11.11   CONTAINER PRE-PULL

It is important to 'gate out' a container in time, as destination demurrage fees may otherwise be applied. Port storage and demurrage charges can quickly add up and become unmanageable, especially when importing a large number of containers. The only time containers should remain longer in port is when there is congestion at the unloading site and there are still a certain amount of free days left.

One of the ways to mitigate these types of fees is through pre-pulling containers, defined as an arrangement where an import container is moved from the port to an interim storage area outside of the port, in order to avoid port storage and demurrage charges. It could be cheaper than leaving the container at the port, hence may be used strategically to save costs in certain scenarios, say, when the free days from carriers and ports are about to end or until the consignee is able to receive them for unloading.

At the end of the day, there is no free lunch. Pre-pulling containers from the port may not always be the right choice as staging and storing take space; loading, unloading and re-loading containers cost money.

As stated earlier, pre-pulling is advantageous if you're trying to avoid demurrage and port charges, as it can be used as a strategy to save costs. However, there are also other ways and strategies that you can adopt to not only save demurrage and port storage charges, but also reduce the amount of pre-pulling required.

These are:

- Shipment planning

- Shipment, supply chain visibility and tracking

- Negotiating demurrage terms - ocean carriers or freight forwarders

- Working with 3PLs or 4PLs - to organise shipment planning process, a critical step in supply chain management.

11.12 DRAYAGE

Drayage involves moving cargo over short distances, often within the same urban area or from a port to a nearby facility. The term could be used to describe transportation of shipping containers by truck to its final destination, like from port to warehouse. Drayage acts as a bridge between different transportation methods, like ocean freight, rail, and trucking, ensuring a seamless flow of goods. The amount charged towards drayage services is also termed as drayage.

11.13 PORT CHARGES[66]

Port charges are a set of charges levied by the port or terminal which the container passes through. The range of charges cover

---

[66] Source: *How does demurrage, detention and port charges work?* Hariesh Manaadiar,
https://www.shippingandfreightresource.com/demurrage-detention-and-port-charges/

an entire spectrum. In terms of container shipments, port charges may include but not limited to below:

Terminal Handling Charge (THC): It is the charge levied by the port for the loading and discharging of a container from the ship. THC differs from port to port, terminal to terminal around the world and is charged both by the load port and discharge port.

If the cargo is transhipped anywhere along the route, then the transhipment port also levies this charge (THC), but that is paid by the shipping line directly to the port and this quantum is usually included in the ocean freight charged by the line.

Early Arrival Charge: A charge levied by the port for a container that arrives in the terminal before the stacks into which it is to be taken has been opened. The acceptance of early arrival containers is at the discretion of the port/terminal operator.

Late Arrival Charge: The opposite of the above, this charge levied by the port for a container that arrives in the terminal after the stacks into which it is to be taken has been closed.

Shifting charges*: A charge levied by the port for a container that needs to be shifted around within the stacks. This usually happens when a container is brought in for one port/vessel, but there may have been a change of destination or change in ship or the container is required to be inspected.

Restow: It is an action taken during the load/discharge operation of a container ship wherein a container may be taken off the ship from one stow position and put back into the same or different stow position for purposes of cargo operation. This may or may not involve placing the container on the quay.

This charge is usually for the account of the shipping line unless the shipping line is carrying out the restow operation due to a customer's request for say incorrect stowage due to cargo mis-declaration or change of destination.

Amendment/Cancellation: Charge levied by the port/terminal for amending or cancelling any documentation/activity lodged with them. Example would be passing an amending document for change of destination of a container, or the export of that container needs to be stopped etc.

Port Storage: When the containers have been discharged from a ship, they are moved to a container yard. The port provides a free period of storage (not to be confused with the free period demurrage provided by container lines, explained later). This period is the time permitted to the consignee to take care of customs clearance procedures and transportation of the container to a warehouse of his choosing, or to its final destination.

This stage is important to ports as lack of space may cause port congestion and affect port productivity. If the importer does not clear the goods and move the containers in time, the port levies charges towards what is called 'port storage'.

Port storage charge is levied by the port for the prolonged stay of a container at port after expiry of free days. This may be charged for a full container that is uncleared (imports) or a full container yet to be shipped (exports) or for an empty container sitting in the port.

Port storage may also happen for containers that were short shipped (for example a vessel terminates its operations and sails before schedule) or transhipment containers that have been sitting at the port for long awaiting a transhipment vessel.

Ports/terminals offer a range of days free of storage (free days) and this needs to be closely monitored as port charges could run into very heavy amounts.

Lift On/Lift Off: Charge that may be levied by the port for additional handling done for containers that have already been received in the port for export or required to be moved to an area for inspection for imports etc.

Stuffing/Destuffing *of Containers:* Some ports/terminals allow the stuffing (packing)/destuffing (unpacking) of the containers within the port area and charge customers based on the port tariff.

This activity may happen at ports which provide CFS services and allow containers to be packed or unpacked in the port or due to some mistakes when the cargo was originally packed – say incompatible hazardous cargoes packed together.

Depending on the port/terminal/country, the port charges may be charged directly to the customer (importer or exporter) or to the shipping line, who in turn will charge this to the customer (importer or exporter).

11.14 BUNKER, BUNKERING

In the ancient times steamships used the power of steam to travel. Steam was generated by feeding coal into the furnaces on board the ships. The storage containers for coal was known as a 'bunker'. Since coal was the original fuel for steamships, the term bunker became synonymous with fuel and therefore 'bunker' is simply nothing but 'fuel' (oil) used in ships. Bunkers are supplied through various means such as bunker barges, pipelines, road tankers etc. This depends on the port in question and the accessibility to the ship. The act of supplying a ship with bunkers (fuel) is known as 'bunkering'.

11.15 TRANSLOADING

Transloading refers to the process of transporting containers, cargo, or freight from one method of transportation (say, vessel or airplane) to another (say, railcar or truck-bed). Transloading is recommended when more than one mode of transportation is required for the entire duration of the shipment.

11.16 TRANSHIPMENT

It is the act of off-loading a container from one vessel (generally at a hub port) and loading it onto another vessel for further transportation to the final port of discharge. Cargoes that have been off-loaded at a port for transhipment are NOT allowed to exit the port by land or rail across international borders to a land locked country unless they are declared as Cargo in Transit (CIT). See next.

11.17   CARGO IN TRANSIT (to …name of country)

A cargo that is moved from an origin point across international borders to another country over land is termed as 'Cargo in Transit'. Bills of lading and manifest for cargoes bound for such inland country destinations must carry the clause *Cargo in transit to…(name of country).* In some cases, shipping lines or government regulations might dictate/insist that the clause reads as "Cargo in transit to …. (name of country or final destination) on client care, risk and cost". This clause tells the gateway/transit port/country that the cargo is not meant for consumption in their country and is meant for the manifested inland country and by virtue of this clause, the cargo may be allowed to transit international borders under customs control.

If this clause is not included in the bill of lading and manifest, the movement across the international border will not be allowed and the recipient might need to customs-clear the goods at the gateway port – which might not be an ideal situation for the recipient.

Cargoes in transit may be moved via any mode of transportation depending on the infrastructure available.

The documentation and customs clearance processes between the countries depend on their trade and other co-operation agreements. Unions and Communities such as EU and SADC have agreements for cargoes moving 'in transit' within/via their territories.

11.18 RAMP

It designates the price of transport to a given point, including the loading or unloading of the wagon. It is a classic term in container transport in the United States, most particularly for container rail junctions in Chicago. It should be noted that this term does not include the reloading or unloading on to a road transport unit for local delivery.[67]

11.19 CONTAINER SHUNTING

This is defined as moving empty or laden containers between two points, typically within a relatively short distance to a predefined location. Shunting is often practised for container movements within the port area, moving cargo between the port and an inland depot or within manufacturing plants and warehouse yards.

The primary objective of shunting is to maximize container movements and throughput between two locations, as well as to optimize limited yard space. These movements can happen via road (truck), rail (train) and even sea (barge).[68]

11.20 CROSS DOCKING

Cross docking is the process by which containers are transferred from one transport to another with minimal intervention, with staging and warehousing taking place at the destination where the

---

[67] Source: https://market-insights.upply.com/en/liner-terms-understanding-shipping-companies-rate-offers

[68] Source: https://www.freightcourse.com/pre-pull/

products are ultimately sold. This reduces central warehouse requirements and means that products take less time to make their way to shelves.

CHAPTER 12

CONTAINER SHIPPING

12.1 STAGES IN INTERNATIONAL SHIPPING[69]

The seven stages of international shipping may be broadly classified as:

i.   Export haulage,

ii. Origin handling,

iii. Export customs clearance,

iv. Ocean freight,

v.   Import customs clearance,

vi. Destination handling and

vii. Import haulage.

---

[69] Source: https://www.worldtradia.com/cargo-shipment-process/

12.1.1 HAULAGE

Haulage refers to the transportation of goods by road or rail from one place to another. In the context of our deliberation on container movement, the term usually refers to transportation from a port to an inland warehouse or factory or vice-versa. The responsibility for this kind of transportation may be undertaken by the merchant exporting or importing a consignment. This is known as 'merchant haulage'. Alternately, for 'carrier haulage', the operation is carried out by the carrier itself.

The main differences between the two relate to their own infrastructure at the point of export or import, transport costs, control over operations and overall capability with regard to their supply chain efficiency. The issues relate to (a) cost management, (b) operational control, (c) risk and reliability, and (d) capability and resources.

The merchant would have to apply its mind seriously to all these issues and decide whether it would be capable of carrying out the entire supply chain management efficiently on its own, or be better off if it relied on the carrier to manage the haulage. (In this context recall the sharing of responsibilities against the "D" terms under the Incoterms 2020 rules.)

12.1.2 EXPORT HAULAGE

It involves the transfer of the cargo from the shipper to the freight forwarder's location (a warehouse or a CFS) the goods being transported by road (truck), rail or an inland waterway. Where the importer arranges for a freight forwarder to manage the transportation of the goods from the seller's premises to the buyer's, the importer's forwarder contacts its overseas partner to arrange collection of the goods. The overseas representative will in turn contact the relevant supplier and arrange for the export of the goods. Otherwise it's the seller who arranges for the export haulage operation.

12.1.3 ORIGIN HANDLING

Origin handling covers all physical handling and inspection of the cargo from its reception at the originating warehouse till it is loaded on a ship. It is always the freight forwarder contracted for the international shipping who is responsible for performing the origin handling. It starts with cargo receiving where the cargo is unloaded from the truck it arrives on and put in a staging area where it is counted and inspected. The cargo is validated against the booking details and the forwarder's cargo receipt is issued to the shipper documenting that the cargo has been received for shipping.

Origin handling of a LCL container: The cargo will then be placed in a stack in the origin warehouse for consolidation with other shipments intended to load into one container for the same destination port. A few days before vessel departure, the shipments are stuffed into the shipping line's container, and the container trucked to the port. At the port, the container is stacked together with other containers intended to load on the same ship, and finally loaded when the ship is ready in the port.

12.1.4 EXPORT CUSTOMS CLEARANCE

Customs declaration formalities – involving the development and submission of declaration documents to the authorities – are carried out by agencies that have valid customs licenses. These are called customs house brokers.

The export customs clearance can either be performed by a freight forwarder with a valid license or an agent appointed by the freight forwarder. Alternatively, it can be done by a customs house broker appointed directly by the shipper.

12.1.5 OCEAN FREIGHT

The freight forwarder selects a shipping line as carrier. The freight forwarder and the shipping line have a contract of carriage for the cargo, and the shipper or consignee in this case is not subject to any direct interaction with the shipping line.

Ocean freight, however, is never the entire costs of shipping from port to port. There are multiple surcharges levied in the industry, such as bunker adjustment factor and currency adjustment factor, which will all be passed on to the shipper or the consignee. The sales contract should take note of these.

12.1.6 IMPORT CUSTOMS CLEARANCE

Authorities in the destination country require import customs clearance for all cargo moving into the country. The process needs to be completed before the cargo enters the country. The import customs clearance process must be completed prior to the cargo leaving a customs bonded area in the country of destination. Import customs clearance is performed by the freight forwarder or an agent of the freight forwarder, by a licensed customs house broker or a CHA (customs house agent) appointed by the consignee (as long as they hold a valid license).

12.1.7 DESTINATION HANDLING

It is a process carried out at destination before the cargo can be released to a consignee. In short, destination handling includes transfer of the container from the ship to shore and from the port to the forwarder's destination warehouse. It also includes un-stuffing of the container and preparation of the cargo collection by the consignee.

12.1.8 IMPORT HAULAGE

The transfer of the cargo from the import warehouse to the consignee address and to the cargo's final destination is referred to as import haulage. It would usually be by truck or a combination of truck and train, and can take from a few hours to many days, depending on the distance and the geography/terrain.

Import haulage can be performed either by the freight forwarder anyway handling the international ocean freight or by a local trucking company. Alternatively, the consignee might decide to collect the cargo himself or herself directly at the destination warehouse.

12.2   STEVEDORING

Stevedoring technically means "from the first point in the ship's or ship's hold to the first point on the quay or vice versa". It is therefore the process of loading or discharging/offloading of cargo to/from a ship.

12.3   CONTAINER MOVEMENT

Over 80% of international trade by volume, or 11 billion tonnes, is done by sea. In terms of value, maritime trade or the international shipping process accounts for goods worth $4.5 trillion annually, according to industry estimates. Today, about 90% of non-bulk cargo worldwide is transported by container ships.

12.3.1 Transhipment of containers

With containers the carriage by the container shipping line commences, at the latest, at the moment the container is "gated in" to the originating terminal. If it was booked say as LCL, or as an FCL packed at the seller's premises and with the forwarder as an NVOCC, then that physical carriage commences at the seller's premises. That container will then be brought by rail or road to the wharf where it will be moved by container handling equipment and loaded on board the vessel by massive cranes.

The contract of carriage for containers usually commences at the seller's premises and is between the seller (freight prepaid) or buyer (freight collect) and a forwarder who sub-contracts for trucking and/or rail to the CY, and the shipping line itself.

Why does transhipment happen? For several reasons, some of which are as follows:

- No direct service between ports;

- Destination port cannot accommodate mega vessels;

- Cost saving, direct shipping usually being costly;

- Intermodal transportation;

- Political or legal restrictions;

Small ports sometimes can be inaccessible for container vessels (low draft, low tide). Hence some of the larger carriers carry on board their own barge (Lighter Aboard SHip or LASH). This is lowered outside such a port and the container lowered onto it for travel into that small port. Some ports have their own barges which go out to meet the container vessel off-shore.

For bulk shipment transhipment is almost impossible because of the very nature of the cargo. Otherwise, transhipment is practically inevitable in container shipments. Container lines schedule their vessels on a hub and spoke basis so containers very often travel on two or more vessels consecutively.

The very nature of the movement of containers dictates that more likely than not, transhipment will take place somewhere along the way, possibly more than once. Most carriers do not even show transhipment on their BLs. Bankers mostly only see the shipping line's CY/CY BL. For container shipment, "transhipment prohibited" in an LC makes no sense, and is futile. Article 20(c)(i)

& (ii) of UCP 600 is very clear about the ground realities, but how many bankers or applicants are aware of this?

Ports of Singapore, Shanghai, Shenzhen, Hong Kong and Busan are some of busiest hubs in international shipping.

12.3.2 The journey – at a glance

The following steps summarise how a container moves from the seller to the buyer.

1. Buyer/importer identifies the need for a product and floats an enquiry in the international market.

2. Sellers/exporters respond with quotations, samples, specifications.

3. Buyer/importer selects from the quotes and reverts;

4. Terms of sale negotiated; shipment terms, delivery terms, payment terms etc. finalised; sales contract executed between seller and buyer.

5. If it's a LCL shipment, the goods will be transported by the seller to the CFS for customs clearance and stuffing. (Go to para #8 next.)

6. If it's a FCL shipment and meant to be stuffed/loaded at the seller's premises, then the freight forwarder picks up 'delivery order' for container from shipping line.

7. Freight Forwarder brings container to seller's/exporter's location inland for its stuffing and sealing under Customs

supervision. It also submits documentation about the shipment to the container shipping line for onward submission of the 'manifest data' to the government authorities – both in the exporting and the importing countries.

8. Freight Forwarder arranges for carriage of container by land transport (truck or rail) from the seller's location inland to the CY for later transportation to the port of loading.

9. Intermodal transporter hands over shipment at port warehouse.

10. CHA arranges for customs clearance, physical examination of the shipment, document verification and payment of port dues. (It should be noted that every country has different requirements for export customs clearance. These can easily be handled on the seller's behalf by a licensed customs broker and freight forwarder.)

11. CHA collects BL after handing over documents and mate's receipt to the shipping line.

12. Port/dock workers load the container on the scheduled carrier.

13. Exporter/seller couriers the original BL and other documents to the importer/consignee. (No bank, LC or

negotiation of documents envisaged in this narrative; otherwise the storyline would have to be modified.)

14. A few days before the ship is scheduled to arrive at the destination port, the captain of the ship provides a report to the concerned authorities of the destination country about the ship, its crew and cargo.

15. Importer/CHA presents the documents to the Customs at the destination port for import clearance.

16. Buyers generally cannot collect their containers even from alongside the vessel at the discharge port. The containers go to the destination CY – maybe some distance from the wharf – where Customs might choose to x-ray them and do other checks before release. Customs officials may select specific container(s) for further inspection. Once cleared by Customs, dock workers load the container on to a special truck or chassis.

The contracted sea freight charges include all components until the container is lifted by the destination terminal equipment from the arriving truck or train at the destination CY and placed in the stack. From that point on, THCD is for the buyer.

17. Importer/buyer/clearing agent arranges for the transportation of the containerised goods to a CY or CFS. If at a CY, the importer or his agent, or a freight forwarder nominated by the buyer (or by the seller if it's on DDP

Incoterms) receives the container for onward transportation to the buyer's place of choice or as previously determined.

[Alternate scenario: Where the shipment is on LCL basis, the container would not be travelling to the buyer's place of choice inland, but end up at a CFS where it will be de-consolidated.]

18. Importer/buyer arranges for the de-stuffing of the container. Hands over empty container at the appointed yard of the shipping line. Delay may attract detention charges.

The above is a general outline of the movement of a container. The sharing of charges and responsibilities – depending on the Incoterms rule selected – is not considered here because if so attempted, the outline above would undergo at least 11 variations. For example, if DDP terms were applied to this narrative, there would have to be a slight change in detail. It would be the *seller's* agent (forwarder) who would be responsible for Customs clearance and the transportation of the container from the arrival CY to the buyer's named location, and for the return of the empty container thereafter to the designated place.

Same with FCA and the other Incoterms 2020 rules.

[Comment: There are Incoterms rules which would in the usual course require the seller to arrange transport of an FCL to a destination CY: namely, CPT, CIP, DAP, DPU, DDP.

If we then look at *delivery* at the destination CY, the possibilities are limited to DAP and DDP, meaning delivered not unloaded. DPU requires the *goods* to be unloaded from the container and that cannot be done in a CY. – Bob Ronai]

CHAPTER 13

CONTAINER SHIPPING AND THE INCOTERMS 2020 RULES

13.1 THE INCOTERMS 2020 RULES

The Incoterms 2020 rules continue to emphasize which of the rules may be used for container transport. The Incoterms rules FAS, FOB, CFR and CIF are meant exclusively for inland waterways and ocean transport. These are not be used for carriage of goods in containers by ship or by air. These rules (barring, of course, FAS) are to be used only where the seller is in a position to deliver the goods *on board* the vessel such as for bulk or break bulk shipment.

Containers are delivered to the carrier at an inland port or at a yard at the port of departure, where the transporter takes over the responsibility for the container's carriage to the destination port. Similar is the story for air cargo.

But what complicates the issues is the definition of "delivery" (clauses A2, B2 in THE Incoterms 2020 rules) when read in conjunction with the modes of transport, the nature of shipment (viz., FCL, LCL, CY/CY, CFS/CFS and so on) and the responsibilities of the seller and the buyer respectively.

13.2   Reason why maritime rules are not used for container shipments

The usual answer is because delivery occurs, and risk transfers, when the goods leave the seller's direct control, such as when the goods are loaded into the container at the seller's premises or at the CFS, long before the goods go on board the carrying vessel. This would be the case with FCA, CPT and CIP.

By the Incoterms definition, risk is transferred with delivery. But for several Incoterms rules, risk continues with the seller even after the seller has lost all control over the shipment as stated in the foregoing because, technically as defined in the Incoterms rules, "delivery" is yet to occur.

Typical examples are the "D" rules in the Incoterms. Here the goods in containers leave the seller's possession, head off overseas entirely outside of the seller's direct control, *yet* "delivery" occurs, and risk transfers, later on in the destination country.

How safe is it for the seller under the Incoterms 2020 rules?

The parties, therefore, need to be careful while contracting for carriage and the selection of the correct ICC Incoterms rules.

Robert (Bob) Ronai, a member of the Drafting Group for the ICC Incoterms 2020 posed the following question through the 'Incoterms' Group previously managed by him on Linkedin:

1. Can the seller deliver DPU destination CY for FCL?

2. Can one use DAP Airport or DAP terminal for LCL shipment?

3. In a CPT contract seller agrees to deliver by 31 March. The seller delivers the goods in loose form on 30 March to its carrier to consolidate as LCL. Payment is by LC calling for an on board B/L and latest shipment period 31 March. Do you see any problems here, and what are they?

4. In an FCA transaction, who pays the costs of a pre-shipment inspection of the goods?

5. DAP requires a named place of destination to be stated. While the rule says nothing more, it is usually accepted that the destination may either be a terminal or the buyer's nominated place.

    Q: If the named place of destination for an airfreight is the airport terminal, can you explain how this rule works in real life?

6. In the Incoterms(r) 2020 DAP rule, does the seller have to take out insurance cover under Institute Cargo Clauses (A)?

The answers are available at the Linkedin > Incoterms Group forum.

Invaluable in content, a series of posts authored by 'Bob' Ronai, interpreting "delivery" (Incoterms rules) – especially by containers – is also available at the same website. Familiarity with these would go a long way in attaining conceptual clarity as far as the ICC Incoterms 2020 rules (vis-à-vis container shipment and 'delivery' as applicable) are concerned.

13.3   GAFTA

Grain and Feed Trade Association (GAFTA) is an international trade association with over 1900 members in 98 countries. Its aim is to promote international trade in agricultural commodities - and more recently spices and general produce. Eighty percent of world trade with grains is said to be regulated under GAFTA-conditions.

GAFTA also uses terms such as CIF, C&F, CIFFO, C&FFO, and FOB. Unlike the Incoterms rules, terms such as FOB, C&F, CIF, Ex Store and FCA are used with reference to container shipment. Bulk shipment of food grain may often be under CIF or C&F terms under GAFTA, which are *not* the Incoterms rules. The following, among others, do not apply to contracts under GAFTA:

- The United Nations Convention on Contracts for the International Sale of Goods of 1980.

- The United Nations Convention on Prescription (Limitation) in the International Sale of Goods of 1974 and the amending Protocol of 1980.

- Incoterms 2020 rules.

The GAFTA terms are defined under articles which have no similarity with the Incoterms rules. Therefore, banks should be extra careful while handing out their standard LC application forms that have pre-printed Incoterms options for the importer to select from. Issuing banks should not confuse the GAFTA rules with the terms under Incoterms 2020 rules, and hence need to be clear about what their importer/customer really wants when they select a three-letter expression.

Banks should take care to update their application forms for LCs so that all the current options are made available through the application form to the applicants for their information and selection while filling up the forms. The application forms should be so designed that data transfer to the SWIFT MT7XX series is practically seamless.

CHAPTER 14

REVISION EXERCISE

(Answer stating reasons wherever necessary, along with exceptions or variations as may be applicable.)

1. Is CY/CY shipment equivalent to (i.e. synonymous with) port-to-port shipment? Any exceptions.

2. Is CFS/CFS shipment equivalent to (i.e. synonymous with) a port-to-port shipment? Any exceptions?

3. Is a FCL or a LCL container allowed to be stuffed or de-stuffed at a CY? If not, where is it done?

4. Is bulk cargo usually transported by containers? What about break bulk cargo?

5.   Can the term FOB Incoterms 2020 be used for the shipment of bulk cargo?

6.   Where a consignment is delivered "free out", is the cost of unloading from the carrying vessel at the destination port included in the freight charged?

7.   What does FIFO mean? Who bears the loading and unloading charges where this term is applied?

8.   What are refrigerated containers called? How is the internal temperature controlled during transit?

9.   How is dry bulk cargo packed for the purpose of transportation by an ocean going vessel?

10.   What is a fully dedicated container carrying ship (ship meant for transporting only containers) called?

11.   In what respects is a ro-ro vessel different from a lo-lo vessel?

12.   What are "liner terms"? Give a few examples.

13.   'When booking cargo on FIOS terms the ship bears responsibility for the speed of loading or discharging'. Is the statement correct? Please explain.

14.   What's the difference between a port and a harbour, a harbour and a jetty?

15.   Distinguish between a container port, a container yard and a container terminal.

16.   Define these terms: LIFO, LILO, FLT, FIOS.

17.   In the case of a CY/CY shipment, the carrier's responsibilities begin and end at which points?

18.   Where does Customs clearance and de-stuffing take place for FCL and LCL shipments respectively?

19.   Explain the difference between "demurrage" and "detention". Do these terms apply to LCL shipment? Give reasons for your answer.

20.   What is a freight terminal? In what ways is it different from a CFS?

21.   Who can own and operate a container terminal? Could a carrier company be permitted to do so?

22.   What is an 'Off Dock CY'? Is it the same as an ICD?

23.   Empty containers are usually held in a _________ before their next use. (Options: container yard, container depot, container port, container freight station, any other?).

24.   Differentiate between a dry port and an ICD (inland container depot).

25.   A container yard is primarily used for which type of shipment – FCL or LCL?

26.   Is it correct that FCL describes a container shipment that must be loaded to its full capacity? Up to what percentage

of its internal capacity is to be utilised for the shipment to be called a FCL shipment?

27. What is the difference between a LCL and a FCL container? Can a LCL container be stuffed to its full capacity?

28. Differentiate between a dry port and a CFS.

29. What is the difference between a 'maritime container terminal' and an 'inland terminal'?

30. Is there any difference between a 'dry port' and an 'inland port'? If yes, what are they?

31. A groupage operator issues which type of transport document to the individual shippers, a HBL (house bill of lading) or a MBL (master bill of lading)? What's the difference?

32. When a groupage operator makes a shipment, is it booked with the carrier as a FCL or a LCL shipment? Which B/L is issued by the carrier - a CY/CY, CFS/CFS or CY/CFS?

33. Where the term FCL/LCL is used, does it indicate a CY/CFS, CY/CY, or CFS/CFS shipment?

34. A FCL shipment is earmarked for "destination CY". Would DPU Incoterms 2020 be appropriate under the circumstances?

35.   What is the difference between "consolidation" and "stuffing"?

36.   Is a house bill of lading (HBL) a document of title?

37.   What do you understand by the term "export haulage"?

38.   Which are the Incoterms 2020 rules that may be used for shipment by container?

39.   Which of the Incoterms 2020 rules are best suited for container transportation under LCs? Explain why the others are not.

40.   Are containers necessary for the bulk shipment of grain? Why?

41.   Why are these Incoterms rules 2020 viz., FOB, CFR and CIF not for LCL or FCL shipments?

42.   What is "GAFTA"? In what way(s) is it different from the Incoterms 2020 rules?

43.   What is the difference between "dwell time" and "lay time"?

44.   Demurrage and detention do not apply to LCL shipments. These are applicable only for FCL shipments. Please explain.

45.   Explain the difference between "segregation" and "deconsolidation".

46.   'An FCL/LCL shipment is supposed to be delivered to a CFS at destination'. Is the statement correct? If 'yes', why the destination must be CFS and not a CY.

47.   A credit requires the B/L to show that shipment was in FCL container. The B/L shows goods being shipped in containers, but marked as CY/CY. Does the latter marking satisfy the requirement of the L/C?

48.   What is the difference between the terms CFR-LO and CFR-FO?

49.   What is a 'geared' carrier? What are its advantages?

50.   When the terms "Panamax" and "Supermax" are used, what are we talking about?

51.   What could be the reasons for difference in transit time between FCL and LCL cargo from the same departure point to the same destination?

52.   In a shipment on EXW Incoterms 2020, who should arrange and pay for securing the cargo in a container?

ANNEXURES

DEMURRAGE, DETENTION AND PORT CHARGES CALCULATION SCENARIO[70]

Scenario: A container is discharged off a ship on the 2nd July. Consignee takes release of the cargo from the port on 12th July and returns the empty to the nominated depot on the 19th of July.

- Demurrage free days offered by the shipping line = 7 days

- Detention free days offered by the shipping line = 10 days

- Free days at port = 3 days

Demurrage calculation example:

As per above dates, on the 12th July, the box would have been sitting in the port/terminal for a total of 11 days.

As per above scenario, line free days for demurrage will expire on the 8th of July.

11 days dwell time – 7 free days = 4 days that the box has overstayed its welcome in the port/terminal.

So, the line will be eligible to charge the consignee **DEMURRAGE** for four days from 9th to 12th July at a rate fixed by the line.

---

[70] Reprinted with permission from author – Hariesh Manaadiar, https://www.shippingandfreightresource.com/demurrage-detention-and-port-charges/

Detention calculation example:

The full container moves out of port on the 12th, the customer returned the empty only on the 19th of July.

Detention free days = 10 days so this is valid till the 21st of July, but since the customer returned the empty on the 19th of July, **DETENTION** charges do not apply.

Port storage calculation example:

Using above dates, since the port only offers 3 free days which expired on the 04 July, then there will be 8 days of **port storage** till the 12th of July to be paid along with the demurrage.

So in essence for this container, the customer would pay:

- Demurrage = 4 days (2nd July to 8th July is free, demurrage from 9th July to 12th July) – to the shipping line

- Detention = 0 days (10 days free so 12th July to 21st July is free, empty returned on 19th July so no detention)

- Port Storage = 8 days (2nd July to 4th July falls under port free days, so from 5th July to 12th July, 8 days of storage applicable) – to the port directly or via the shipping line

Combined demurrage/detention calculation example:

In above example, if "combined demurrage/detention" principle was to be used, then,

- 7 line free days ends 8th July;

- Container moves out on the 12th July and empty returned on the 19th July;

- So there will be Demurrage/Detention for 11 days payable to the shipping line.

The various scenarios should now be clear to the reader.

- Port Storage = 8 days (2nd July to 4th July falls under port free days, so from 5th July to 12th July, 8 days of storage applicable) – to the port directly or via the shipping line

If you request additional line free days from the shipping line they may ask if it is for demurrage or detention. In various destination ports, the definition of demurrage and detention varies and hence the line needs to know where their exposure lies.

If the free days is shown as just "free days" it usually refers to "combined demurrage/detention" which is what a lot of the shipping lines apply to keep the calculations simple.

- *If "x" free days is offered for demurrage only, then that means that the client has "x" free days to pick up the full container after which the empty has to be returned the same day to avoid costs.*

- *If "x" free days is offered for detention only, then that means that the client can use the "x" free days to unpack the container and take it back to the depot. They might have some unpacking problems at their warehouse which necessitates such requests.*

RESOURCE CENTRES AND ACKNOWLEDGEMENTS:

1. Linkedin Group page on the Incoterms 2020 rules:
https://www.linkedin.com/groups/3347103/

2. Linkedin Group page on Trade Finance:
https://www.linkedin.com/groups/140671/

3. Blog page of Kim Sindberg:
https://lcviews.com/index.php

4. Blog page of David Meynell:
https://www.tradefinance.training/

5. A glossary of maritime terms:
https://www.maritimeinfo.org/en/Glossary/

6. Shipping and Freight Resources:
https://www.shippingandfreightresource.com/

7. Trade Services Update: www.tradeservicesupdate.com

8. Supply chain related content:
https://www.freightcourse.com/

9. Richard (Bob) Ronai, former owner of Incoterms Group on Linkedin with 66,000+ members

10. Grateful thanks to a host of other sources acknowledged (as far as possible) by way of footnotes, and others that were not acknowledged. Thanks for lending me your shoulders.

FCL SHIPMENT

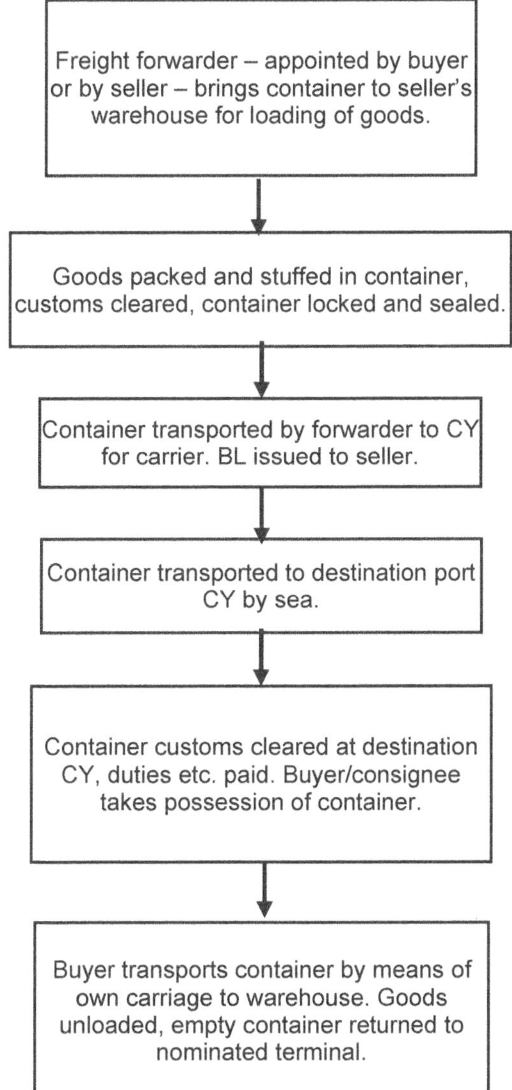

LCL SHIPMENT

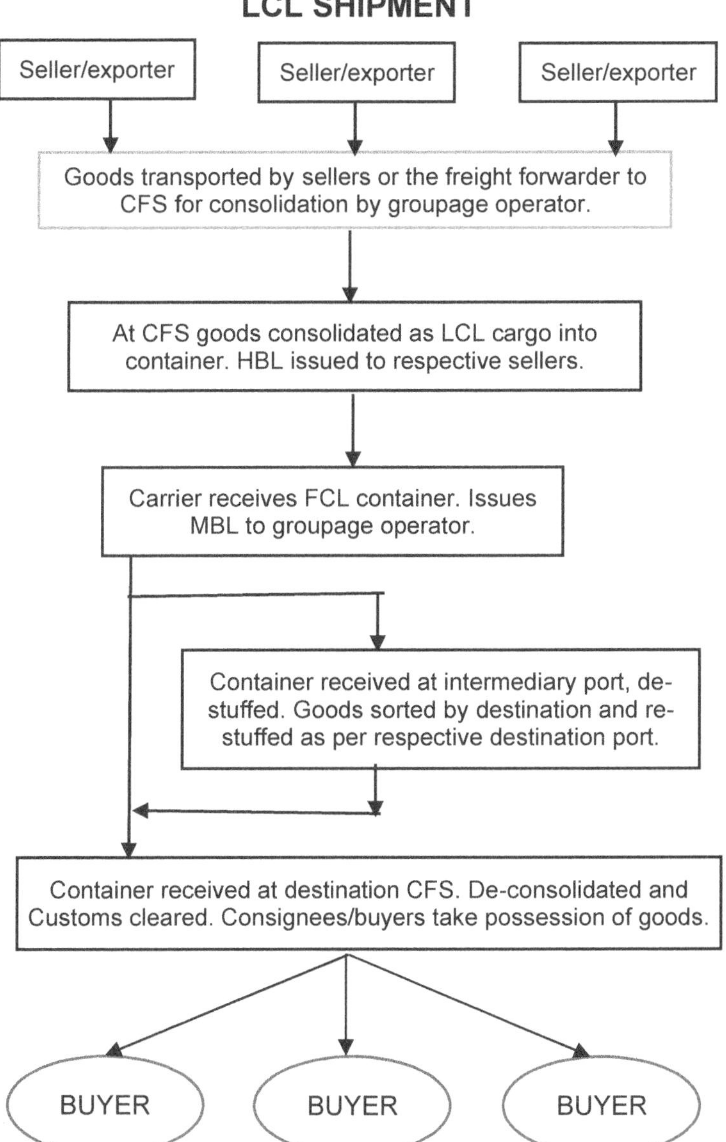

MULTIMODAL BILL OF LADING EXAMPLE

SHIPPER: TAKATA SHIPPING AND TRADING LLC THE FREEMEN BUILDINGS SUITE 106, 2501 COPPERSIDE ROAD, WILMINGTON DE 16800, USA	**BILL OF LADING** PORT TO PORT OR COMBINED TRANSPORT
CONSIGNEE: THE BANK OF TOKYO-MITSUBISHI UFJ, LTD.	**BILL OF LADING NO:** FSCU1303201800001ZM150 **NUMBER OF ORIGINALS:** 1/3
NOTIFY: KEN&RYU TRADING CO., LTD. 1-2-3 KAWAHARA, HIRAKATA, OSAKA	**FAST STARS LINE SHIPPING COMPANY S.A.**

VESSEL AND VOYAGE: MSC SEATTLE - NL739R	PLACE OF RECEIPT: BATON ROUGE, LOUISIANA, USA	PORT OF LOADING: THE NEW ORLEANS PORT, USA
BOOKING REFERENCE: 082MERI1020030	PORT OF DISCHARGE: PORT OF OSAKA, JAPAN	PLACE OF DELIVERY:

CONTAINER NOS	DESCRIPTION OF GOODS AND PACKAGES	GROSS WEIGHT
SEGU5175079/40HC	SOYBEAN IN BULK FREIGHT PREPAID. LETTER OF CREDIT NO: EXP180253 SHIPPED ON BOARD AT THE NEW ORLEANS PORT, USA ON VESSEL MSC SEATTLE - NL739R ON 13.MARCH.2018. PRE-CARRIAGE BY TRUCK.	21000,000KGS

RECEIVED by the Carrier from the Shipper in apparent good order and condition unless otherwise indicated herein, the Goods, or package(s) said to contain the Goods, to be carried subject to all the terms and conditions herein. Delivery of the Goods to the Carrier for Carriage hereunder constitutes the Merchant's acceptance of all the stipulations, exceptions, terms and conditions of this Bill as fully as if signed by him, any contrary local custom or privilege notwithstanding. This Bill supersedes all prior agreements or freight engagements for the Goods. In witness whereof, the undersigned, on behalf of the Carrier, has signed the number of Bills stated hereunder, all of this tenor and date. Where issued as a Bill of Lading, delivery may be made against only one original Bill in which case, the others shall stand void.	**SHIPPED ON BOARD DATE:** 13.MARCH.2018 **PLACE OF ISSUE:** NEW ORLEANS, USA **AS CARRIER** FAST STARS LINE SHIPPING COMPANY S.A. (Signature)

Usage of the terms FCL, LCL etc. in BLs:

Consignor

WEIDMANN SYSTEMS INTERNATIONAL
NEUE JONASTRASSE 60 CH-8640
RAPPERSWIL SWITZERLAND

FBL   061565   TR

NEGOTIABLE FIATA
MULTIMODAL TRANSPORT
BILL OF LADING
Issued subject to UNCTAD/ICC Rules for
Multimodal Transport Documents (ICC Publication 481).

Consigned to order of

FEDERAL TRANSFORMERS CO. LLC,
P.O.BOX 9769,
ABU DHABI
UNITED ARAB EMIRATES

Notify address

SAME AS CONSIGNEE

Ref.No: 2.1.82.02.517-0000549

For delivery of goods please apply to:
JUMA AIRLINK L.L.C.
OFFICE #B1, MEZZANINE FLOOR
MUBARAK BIN HAMOODAH BLDG.
AL NASR STREET ABU DHABI
P.O.BOX 27374

Place of receipt

Ocean vessel   Port of loading   ISTANBUL

GRAND 2333
Port of discharge   Place of delivery   ISTANBUL

ABU DHABI

Marks and numbers	Number and kind of packages	Description of goods	Gross weight	Measurement
	S.T.C.		244.000-KG	
PONU/153982/0	2 CASES			

800 PCS 511308-A3 KSSA OIL LEVEL INDICATOR
ORDER NO: 7002662

-LCL/LCL
-FREIGHT PREPAID
-SHIPPERS LOAD, COUNT & STOW

-THE GOODS ARE LOADED INTO CONTAINER ON 15.11.2002

according to the declaration of the consignor

Declaration of interest of the consignor
in timely delivery (Clause 6.2.)

****

Declared value for ad valorem rate according to
the declaration of the consignor (Clauses 7 and 8)

****

The goods and instructions are accepted and dealt with subject to the Standard Conditions printed overleaf.

Taken in charge in apparent good order and condition, unless otherwise noted herein, at the place of receipt for transport and delivery as mentioned above.

One of these Multimodal Transport Bills of Lading must be surrendered duly endorsed in exchange for the goods. In Witness where of the original Multimodal Transport Bills of Lading all of this tenor and date have been signed in the number stated below, one of which being accomplished the other(s) to be void.

Freight amount	Freight payable at	Place and date of issue
Cargo insurance through the undersigned ☐ not covered ☐ Covered according to attached Policy	ISTANBUL Number of Original FBL's	ISTANBUL Stamp and signature
X For delivery of goods please apply to:	3 / THREE	AS AGENTS ONLY SCHENKER ARKAS NAKLIYAT VE TIC. A.Ş.

Shipping line name

BILL OF LADING
ORIGINAL

(4) Notify Party (complete name and address)
SAME AS CONSIGNEE

(13) Place of Receipt/Date
SHANGHAI, CHINA

(14) Ocean Vessel/Voy. No.
I L LAGUNA 087S

(15) Port of Loading
SHANGHAI, CHINA

(16) Port of Discharge
BRISBANE, AUSTRALIA

(17) Place of Delivery
BRISBANE, AUSTRALIA

CONTAINER NO./SEAL NO.

/20'/EMCDKV6419/4 PACKAGES
1 X 20'

CO., LIMITED
CARBON STEEL
FLANGE LFKC1909

CARBON STEEL FLANGE

6.0400 CBM
23,384.000 KGS

"OCEAN FREIGHT PREPAID"
SHIPPER'S LOAD & COUNT
4 PACKAGES

CONTAINERS OR PACKAGES ONE (1) CONTAINER ONLY

AS ARRANGED

ON BOARD

SHANGHAI

THREE (3)

SHANGHAI AUG.22,2019

SHANGHAI

AUG.22,2019
ITAL LAGUNA 087S
SHANGHAI

FCL/FCL 0/0

NOTES